Male and Female He Made Them

MARY JO ANDERSON
ROBIN BERNHOFT, M.D.

Male and Female
He Made Them

Questions and Answers
about Marriage and
Same-Sex Unions

CATHOLIC ANSWERS
SAN DIEGO
2005

Published by Catholic Answers, Inc.
2020 Gillespie Way
El Cajon, California 92020
(888) 291-8000 (orders)
(619) 387-0042 (fax)
www.catholic.com (web)

Cover by Russell Design, Pasadena, California

Printed in the United States of America
ISBN 1-888992-75-1

Contents

Preface

How to Use this Book

This volume was conceived to serve a dual purpose. The publisher sought a user-friendly guide for an urgent matter of public discourse. The goal is to facilitate the widest possible use.

Some readers will find it most helpful to begin at the introduction and read through to the conclusion. Others will find that the format is more useful as a manual for ready references, based on a specific aspect of the debate over same-sex unions, such as "what does science tell us about homosexuality?" or "political considerations."

When used as a reference, these pages need not be read in order. Each numbered question and answer is written as a complete unit to stand on its own without the necessity to read the preceding question for context. In this manner, one may quickly consult the table of contents for the topic of interest and read only those questions and answers that apply to one's own interest. This permits parents, apologists, journalists, radio hosts, pastors, politicians, and doctors to refer to a single issue at the point of need in a given discussion.

The appendices are also a ready resource. Appendix I is a list of the scriptural verses that address homosexual acts. The actual text of the verse is given so that it is not necessary to separately search the Bible while reading this volume. Appendix II offers resources for those who seek additional help for their marriages, issues of fertility, or homosexuality. Appendix III is short list of books and tapes available for those who wish to study the issues in greater depth than they are presented in this volume.

Introduction

This book examines the arguments that surround a crucial social question of our time: What does contemporary culture think about marriage and same-sex unions?

Public discourse interchanges the terms "same-sex marriages," "same-sex partnerships," and "domestic partnerships." Public debate asks, "Is a sexual relationship a civil right? What will same-sex unions mean to national policy, families, and children? How would a culture with multiple models of marriage function?"

The sexual instinct insures the survival of the species by bonding a man and a woman together to build a family. Every culture in all eras has had something to say about cultural norms that govern sex, marriage, and family. Healthy, enduring societies are societies in which the norms of sex, marriage, and family are based on respect for the human person and enjoy a wide consensus.

Today, modern democratic societies struggle to define and refine the meaning of love, sex, marriage, and family in a pluralistic culture. Advanced technologies and competing worldviews have raised new, urgent questions about the nature of sex and marriage that affect every member of the society as well as the future of the culture.

The resolution of the question "Can a new model for marriage include same-sex unions?" touches the powerful connectors that hold a multicultural society together: the common good, tolerance, civil rights, the democratic process, religious freedom, privacy, and freedom of speech. When the question is resolved, it will have an immediate impact on religious practice, public policy, education, and family law.

Essential to this debate are citizens who are well informed about the relationship of marriage and family to society. Catholics believe that God designed sexuality, male and female, to be complementary. Sexuality is God's gift for the unity of husband and wife, who together create a family: the first community. The Catholic Church teaches that the conjugal expression of love is an exclusive gift for one man and one woman joined in the sacrament of holy matrimony. Deep bonds of friendship are also a gift of God for all, married or single. Homosexual persons are due respect and love. They should enjoy genuine, vibrant—but chaste—relationships.

Proposed alternate models of marriage that include same-sex unions must be wisely examined. The goal of this book is to help citizens recover a known but marginalized truth: Marriage and family life ordered to the divine design builds healthy, peaceful communities.

Same-Sex Unions and Society

Why is there an objection to same-sex unions in a modern pluralistic society?

A general answer is that cultural norms are set by accepted practices. If same-sex "marriage" becomes an accepted legal practice, then it will become a cultural norm. Most people recognize that a homosexual lifestyle is not healthy. Therefore it should not become a cultural norm promoted equally with marriage or glamorized in education, art, public policy, entertainment, etc. As such, it would have a devastating impact on every social institution. Hence, it will destroy all pluralities within the culture. Religious freedom and practice will be particularly jeopardized (see q. 133).

Marriage is also a serious public health issue. Marital failure (divorce) is the cause of more damage to the health and longevity of divorced persons than any other *medical* risk factor, including smoking.[1] Additionally, the children of divorced parents exhibit poorer physical and emotional health.[2] It is in the best interest of our societies to foster policies that encourage healthy marriages.

When close to 10 percent of the population is homosexual and is affected by a decision for or against homosexual unions, isn't it fair to accommodate their need to form families?

One hundred percent of the population is affected by a decision for or against same-sex "marriages." We do not segregate neighborhoods or co-workers based on sexual practice.

Two points should be made. First, the figure of 10 percent is highly disputed, even among advocates of homosexual marriages. Ten percent is a political number, designed to give weight to the demands made by a small group of activists. A more accurate figure is 3–5 percent, and some think even that number is generous (see qq. 104–106).

Second, society has no obligation to legally sanction a destructive behavior because a statistically significant portion of the population is engaged in the behavior. To illustrate this point, substitute another behavior—pedophilia—for homosexual acts. Does society have an obligation to legally approve and permit celebration of "unions" of forty-year-old men married to ten-year-old girls or boys if it can be shown that 10 percent of the population has a preference for pedophilia?

Though this particular substitution may be offensive to consider, a legal battle over pedophilia awaits a society that codifies homosexual acts. Already a group called the North American Man-Boy Love Association has begun a push to decriminalize pedophilia and lower the age of consent, and in the Netherlands, homosexual advocates have sought to lower the age of consent to twelve. It is instructive to recall that years before homosexual activists began a movement for legal marriages, they sought decriminalization of homosexual acts.

3

Same-sex unions are a civil matter. Why should religious interests object as long as churches are free to marry people according to their own teachings?

It is curious that those who cherish plurality and argue for cultural diversity reject the participation of religious voices in the public square. Historian James Hitchcock wrote, "Both church and state have a legitimate interest in marriage not to help people celebrate their emotional ties . . . but in order to create stable communities that at least in principle are open to the possibility of children, communities that, as Catholic doctrine has always held, are indeed the indispensable foundation of society."[3]

A Pew Research poll conducted in February 2004 found that Americans reject homosexual "marriages" by more than two to one (65 percent to 28 percent). An earlier poll found that 82 percent of people opposed to homosexual marriages object on religious grounds.[4] Other polls have also identified moral or religious grounds for rejection of homosexual marriages.[5] Clearly a wide majority of Americans oppose same-sex marriages, and the majority of those citizens reject it for religious or moral reasons.

The question could be framed differently: Can a pluralistic culture afford to dismiss so many voices?

4

Is the debate over same-sex unions just one feature of the larger culture war that sets traditional morality against a progressive, pluralistic, democratic worldview?

Broadly, yes. But both sides of the culture war—a progressive, pluralistic democracy and a democracy informed by traditional morality—are best served when their arguments are rooted in truth.

Same-sex unions violate the complementary design of the sexes and are a misuse of the sexual function. The same-sex "marriage" debate must acknowledge objective realities that are non-negotiable, such as the physiological structure and sexual function of human beings. For Catholics, that observable reality is summed up in this scriptural passage: "God created man in his own image . . . male and female he created them. . . . And God said to them, 'Be fruitful and multiply'" (Gen. 1:27–28). The first blessing of God on humankind was the fruitfulness of the man and woman. Their fruitfulness was the genesis of the first communities.

Ultimately, we as a society must make decisions that are best for the whole community, not merely for one group. Homosexual unions are not in the best interests of the whole society. Such unions are also not in the best interest of homosexual persons (see chapter 4).

5

What about the rise of "hate crimes" against homosexuals? Once same-sex partnerships are legally recognized, won't violence against homosexual people stop?

FBI statistics report that violence against homosexual persons by heterosexuals is extremely rare. All claims of an epidemic of "hate crimes" against homosexual persons are a public relations ruse. According to the latest FBI hate crimes statistics, it is estimated that less than 0.0001 percent of homosexuals were victims of violent assaults by heterosexuals.[6]

Homosexual activists who are truly concerned about violence against persons in the "gay lifestyle" would do a great service to speak up about the violence within their lifestyle. The *Journal of Interpersonal Violence* reports that 31 percent of lesbians interviewed admitted to physical abuse by a partner in the preceding year.[7] A similar study found 22 percent of male homosexuals reported physical partner violence.[8] By contrast, married women have the lowest rates of violent abuse by partners.[9]

6

Hasn't society concluded that it is best to keep religious views personal?

Are "do not steal" or "do not murder" views that should remain personal?

These are religious commands, but society recognizes their innate truth. The erroneous assumption is that any viewpoint informed by religious thought should be disallowed in public debate. The question should not be "Is the religious view opposed to the secular view?" but "Is the religious view objectively true?"

7

Shouldn't public space be reserved for rational—not religious—debate?

Former federal circuit court judge Robert Bork wrote, "The idea that men are naturally rational, moral creatures without the need for strong external restraints has been exploded by experience." [10] Bork's observation is proved by the same-sex union debate. The fact is that "rational" is not at the heart of the defense of homosexual unions. If it were, all would reject it, for the lifestyle is dangerous, destructive, and opposed to the stability of society.

A challenge for people of faith is an obligation "to appeal to spiritual and moral capacities of the human person . . . so as to obtain social changes that will really serve him." [11] The difficulty is that where society confuses means (methods, including laws) with ends (to assist people to be healthy and happy), "unjust structures" result that "make Christian conduct in keeping with the commandments of the divine law-giver difficult and almost impossible." [12]

8

Perhaps the question of same-sex unions is moot. Isn't marriage little more than a social construct? Why not reconstruct it to fit current needs?

Marriage, defined as a union of a man and a woman, is innate to human communities; it is not an artificial construct. Anthropologists find some variation of marriage in all cultures throughout history. No sustainable culture has ever been studied that was not organized around a man and a woman and their children in a socially recognized bond. Turned around, history finds no culture in which families are systematically organized according to free association rather than biological kinship.

Samuel Silver, chairman of Toward Tradition, [13] wrote, "Unlike private sexual behavior between consenting adults, same-sex marriage is neither a private matter nor an individual right. It is a social and legal contract that would publicly sanction and promote a lifestyle and set of behaviors that the vast majority of Americans hold as immoral, unhealthy, and/or unnatural. Most base their viewpoint on universal biblical law, but many others understand that sexual morality is also a basic tenet of natural law derived from human nature. It is not a social construct."

9

Objectively—beyond biology—isn't it a secular question of equal rights under the law, not of the sanctity of marriage? Why discriminate against homosexual partners? Don't they deserve the same respect in a pluralistic society as heterosexuals?

Persons with same-sex attraction deserve respect, as do all members of society. The Catholic Church forbids "unjust discrimination" and insists that homosexual persons be "accepted with respect, compassion, and sensitivity." [14] But the Church also teaches that they are called to chastity. [15] This is a standard that the Church enjoins on all single persons (see q. 67).

An emphasis on "rights" and "choice" is nothing less than massive cover for policies that kill and sicken the society. Clarity is crucial: Homosexual acts are medically dangerous and even lethal. That is medicine and science—not "rights" or "choice" or even "religion."

When any group demands "rights," it is well to pause to consider what corresponding responsibilities attend to those rights. The first responsibility is to truth. The objective truth is that males and females are physically ordered to one another. Anyone desirous of a "right" to a sexual relationship has first a responsibility to the truth of human biology.

As for discrimination, current marriage laws do not unjustly discriminate against any citizen in the application of marriage law, regardless of whether the intent of the bond is religious or secular. Any two people who are of age may marry, provided that they marry within the regulations set by law, which requires one man and one woman as parties to the bond.[16]

10

Don't current laws discriminate against homosexual partnerships when they are deprived of the significant economic benefits granted to heterosexual couples?

Homosexual persons, whatever one thinks of the specific behavior, should be protected in civil law the same as any other citizen. But marriage laws do not unfairly discriminate against persons in same-sex relationships, as the homosexual lobby would have the public believe.

If the laws treat homosexual pairs unjustly, then cohabiting heterosexuals could make that identical complaint, as could single college roommates or indeed any self-constituted couple. When viewed objectively, what is proposed is that any pair who is willing to declare some sort of bond should be given economic concessions by the community.

Society has generally seen a benefit to the whole community when certain concessions are made to that unit that renders a particular service to the society: the establishment of families. That service is rendered in the institution of marriage. Marriage laws follow human history, which in turn follows human biology; marriage has always been defined as the exclusive bond of one man and one woman.[17]

11

Haven't recent studies in history uncovered the custom of homosexual marriages in some cultures?

There is no evidence for that claim. There are texts from ancient Near East cultures that describe male cult prostitutes, and homosexuality was not unknown as a feature of certain sects. But their practices were not patterned on marriage. Some scholars have suggested that there is evidence of same-sex "marriages" found in certain manuscripts that are unclear in context.

Male rites of passage or rituals of prowess detailed in some ancient texts have had a homo-erotic interpretation read into them by contemporary activists who seek to "prove" that ancient cultures accepted same-sex unions. According to Peter Lubin and Dwight Duncan, "there is no 'rich history of same-sex marriage that . . . was suppressed in recent Western History and is only now coming to light.'"[18] The ancient world overwhelmingly rejected homosexual practice in emphatic terms as unnatural. The Roman historian Tacitus described Nero's actions as follows: "Nero, who polluted himself by every lawful or lawless indulgence, had not omitted a single abomination that could heighten his depravity, until a few days afterwards he stooped to marry himself to one of that filthy herd, by name Pythagoras, with all the forms of regular wedlock."[19]

12

Why do so many homosexuals point to ancient Greece as an example of a tradition that revered homosexual relationships?

Their claim is mostly revisionist history, but where there were known and tolerated homosexual relationships, it was not a model for marriage. Despite the occasional art on urns, historians have found ancient Greece to be like ancient Everywhere Else: It was dependent on marriage for societal vitality and for its future citizens.

Nikos Vrissimtzis, a sociologist and author of *Love, Sex and Marriage: A Guide to the Private Life of the Ancient Greeks*, said, "Contrary to popular opinion, that world was not a paradise for homosexuals, and paedaracy [pederasty] was held in such contempt that it was very heavily punished." Vrissimtzis spent years in libraries and museums where he studied manuscripts and inscriptions that

detailed Greek life. "Homosexuals were not—as many believed
—openly accepted by society. They were marginalized and punished by law."[20]

13

*John Boswell of Yale University wrote a book detailing ancient Chris-
tian liturgies for same-sex couples.*[21] *Why does the Catholic Church
hide this fact?*

The Church doesn't hide these inspiring ceremonies. The Church,
particularly the Eastern rites, has had and continues to celebrate
"unions" of friends (same sex or opposites).[22] These ceremonies
celebrate platonic friendship and bond the couple as brothers or
brother and sister in a relationship described by another professor
as "stronger than blood, confirmed in the outpouring of the Holy
Spirit. . . . And since it was a spiritual union, it (will) last beyond
the grave."[23]

In reality these ceremonies "solemnify a state—that of friendship—that comes highly recommended in the Christian tradition
('Henceforth I call you not servants . . . but I have called you
friends' [John 15:15])."[24]

Other scholars refute Boswell's claims: "Neither Boswell's re-
construction of them (liturgies) nor his method of argumenta-
tion can possibly support the interpretation he proposes . . . [and]
early Byzantine law codes contain extremely harsh punishments
for homosexual intercourse."[25]

Boswell's concocted history is popular in homosexual activist
circles. Their goal is to justify a change in marriage laws to include same-sex partners by appealing to a supposed ancient practice. This is another feature of the socio-political war on marriage.

14

How can same-sex unions threaten heterosexual marriages? Why not adopt a live-and-let-live approach?

Homosexual partnerships already exist privately in the culture under a live-and-let-live policy.[26] Marriage is a public matter. Its success or failure has a public health and financial impact. It is the movement to *legalize* same-sex unions as a variation of marriage that threatens the structure of our society, the common good, and the attitude of the next generation toward marriage.

The institution of marriage is so crucial that no civilization can afford to dilute or trivialize its meaning or function. Every culture in human history has recognized that the purpose of marriage is to bear, raise, and educate children.[27] Same-sex unions cannot carry out this task, but it can destroy the meaning of marriage and family, which is the essential building block of any nation. Ultimately, a redefinition of marriage to include same-sex unions is a death warrant for a society. For that reason, among others, same-sex "marriages" are a very real threat to society.

15

Why not split the difference and permit same-sex unions to share the legal benefits of marriage but reserve the term **marriage** *for heterosexuals?*

Any legal recognition of same-sex unions is a parody of marriage and as such mocks and trivializes marriage. As a society, we need to strengthen marriages. Furthermore, the portrayal of homosexual activity in the wider culture will become a standard feature of education, media, entertainment—in short, every facet of communal life will be shown to acknowledge homosexual pairs as a normal arrangement. Homosexual acts are gravely immoral[28] and should not be supported as "rightful" in the law or public policy.

In addition, if "domestic partnerships" are legalized, there is no impediment to heterosexual couples registering under such a law.

Respect for marriage would erode under the weight of various options whereby couples could share the legal benefits but not the responsibilities of marriage.

Homosexual activists admit as much. William Eskridge, professor of jurisprudence at Yale Law School, wrote of an emerging "menu" of marriage options: "For example, Canada initially applied its extensive cohabitation rules only to straight couples. But after a ruling by that country's supreme court, the Canadian parliament amended the cohabitation law to include same-sex couples. Whatever the chronological sequence, the result is more couples availing themselves of an option other than marriage. The menu allows partners with a lesser degree of mutual commitment to choose a regulatory regime that offers fewer benefits in return for easier exit from the relationship."[29] In short, even advocates understand that to legalize same-sex "marriages" is to admit that it may lead to fewer marriages among heterosexuals. Society should endeavor to protect and defend the very meaning of marriage, not just the technical definition in law and public policy.

16

How would same-sex unions destroy the meaning of marriage?

First, legalizing same-sex unions formally codifies sex as nothing more than a genital act between consenting adults. It formally separates sex from the unifying embrace of the married couple and their procreative power (see q. 60). Illicit sexual relations of various types have always been an aberration in society, but no culture accepted them as good for the society. No society allowed aberrations to be defined *as marriage* because it threatens procreation, the establishment of families, and the stability of the civilization.

Logic forces a second point. Homosexual partners cannot make a case for their relationship other than personal pleasure. Essentially, if affection and commitment are the "moral" qualifiers for a relationship, then there is no logical line to draw before we slide into polygamy, incest, or incestuous homosexual polygamy for that matter. When society permits persons of the same sex to "marry" based simply on their declaration of love and commitment, there is no reason that three committed persons of the same sex cannot marry.[30]

17

Critics of same-sex unions raise the issue of polygamy as a scare tactic. Who would believe that legalizing same-sex unions leads to polygamy?

Polygamists do, among others. The United States outlawed polygamy in 1878, but grassroots groups are seeking "marriage reform" as part of a "civil rights" battle. Liberal columnists such as Ellen Goodman, Steve Chapman, and Andrew Sullivan have defended polygamy in the *Washington Times*, the *Chicago Tribune*, and other national periodicals.[31]

Michael Heflin, director of OutFront (a project of Amnesty International) and an advocate of same-sex partnerships, insisted that same-sex "marriages" should not be compared to polygamy or bigamy. On the other hand, he conceded, "We don't take a position on bigamy, polygamy or incest. . . . I think these are going to be important debates."[32]

In fact, legalizing same-sex marriages would lead to more than polygamy. Stanley Kurtz of the Hoover Institute warns that the "gradual transition from gay marriage to state sanctioned polyamory (non-monogamous sexual relations between group partners), and the eventual abolition of marriage itself, is now the most influential paradigm within academic family law."[33] Note that Kurtz did not say that it is the paradigm among fringe groups but in academic family law. Clearly, marriage is already under deliberate assault.

18

Why suggest that the legal union of same-sex partners opens the door to group sex? Isn't that a vast overstatement?

Unfortunately, no. When the American Civil Liberties Union came to the defense of Utah polygamist Thomas Green, it supported the repeal of "all laws prohibiting or penalizing the practice of plural marriage."[34] As for polyamory, it has sufficient adherents to publish a magazine called *Love More* and to have public advocates.[35]

Paula Ettelbrick, who has taught a course called "Sexuality and the Law" at the University of Michigan Law School and serves on the National Gay and Lesbian Task Force, champions non-marital family groups—including polyamory—because it will "radically reorder society's view of family."[36]

Ettelbrick declared, "Being queer means pushing the parameters of sex and family, and in the process transforming the very fabric of society."[37] But Ettelbrick does not say what her transformed society will look like. Harvard Law School's Martha Minow is another advocate of a radical redefinition of marriage. She promotes a concept of functional families irrespective of biological ties.[38]

19

Some cultures are polygamous. Is polygamy such a threat to marriage?

Boston Globe columnist Ellen Goodman quipped, "What's the difference between a polygamist, and . . . a casual philanderer? Twenty-five years in prison?"[39] A quick review of all the successful societies in which polygamy is the custom is sufficient warning against permitting that arrangement—because there aren't any. Some ancient cultures did permit forms of polygamy, but the practice was generally abandoned. Even "gay rights" champion Andrew Sullivan is critical of polygamy because it "abuses women, creates a class of unmarried males, and leaves children unclear about their parents."[40]

Sullivan makes a point that the U.S. Supreme Court justices understood in 1878 when they ruled that polygamy "leads to the patriarchal principle," which holds that women are inherently inferior. Naomi Shaefer notes that the government could not sanction a "consensual" polygamy (women have no other choice) any more than it could legalize selling oneself into slavery.[41]

Confusing family bonds erodes the structure of a community. Eugene Volokh, a University of California at Los Angeles law professor and a proponent of same-sex "marriages," predicts that the next logical barrier to be broken is incest. It will be decriminalized despite the dangers of inbreeding, since we do not "ban marriages between people with serious genetic diseases."[42] It takes little reflection on a society in which polygamy and incest are part of the cultural norm to realize that no civilization survives such choices.

20

Perhaps traditional marriage has outlived its utility for pluralistic societies. Why is the success of one meaning of marriage important enough to polarize a nation? We can't legislate morality.

"Polarization" is a tactic of those who propose to make a seismic shift in settled public policy and national culture. Radical experimentation for the sake of disordered passions will destroy the society. Legalizing same-sex unions is not a matter of legislating morality; it is more a matter of legislating an immorality. But, yes, we can and do legislate morality in numerous areas (killing and stealing, for example).

The consensus of mankind has found marriage to be the firm foundation of a healthy culture. Those who defend that broad consensus cannot be faulted for raising the alarm over novelties such as same-sex "marriages." The chaotic vision of multiple models of marriage opens the way for a destructive sexual anarchy. There is in the question a hint of this attitude: "We want sexual anarchy, but we want it to be a civil anarchy, so please do not raise impolite questions."

But it's a matter of national survival. After flexible models of marriage would come "various forms of family," where soon enough children—moving through multiple sets of "parents"—would be little more than wards of the state. The healthy ordering of sexuality is one benefit of marriage that ensures public peace.

21

What other benefits does marriage offer to society?

Marriage and the natural family unit are crucial to the well-being of a civilization as a whole and for each member of the society. Twelve leading scholars on marriage and family compiled recent research data and summarized their findings: "Marriage is an important social good associated with an impressively broad array of positive outcomes for children and adults alike. . . . Building a healthy marriage culture is clearly a matter of legitimate public concern." [43]

Recent studies list the benefits of marriage for the couple, among them physical and mental health, longevity, and prosperity. Divorced and single people have far higher rates of illness, accidents, and depression, and they have shorter life spans. Married persons are more productive. [44] In the reverse, unmarried people are more likely to catch colds and spend time in nursing homes, and unmarried men on average have a life span ten years shorter than married men. These findings hold across a wide range of societies. A 1998 study based on data from seventeen nations found that married people report significantly high levels of happiness. [45]

22

Is the positive data on marriage confined to happy marriages? Wouldn't unhappy marriages balance the so-called benefits of traditional marriage?

The research on marriage was a broad sampling, not separated by categories such as "happy" and "unhappy." Where information is available, the indication is that even "unhappy" marriages are a better environment for people, particularly women and children. Part of the answer lies in a definition of "happy" that is dependent upon the subjective assessment of individuals.

In general, where "unhappy" is understood as dissatisfaction with one or more major factors, such as compatibility or finances (but not with physical abuse or drug and alcohol abuse), married "unhappiness" is transitory, but those marriages still provide a stable, committed partnership. This is borne out in the statistics gathered on children. Pat Fagan of the Heritage Foundation wrote: "For children whose parents remain married . . . the benefits are real. Adolescents from these families have been found to have better health and are less likely to be depressed, are less likely to repeat a grade in school, and have fewer developmental problems. The implications of such mounting evidence for social policy are immense."[46] (These statistics hold true even when children live in homes with "unhappy" marriages.[47])

One benefit of marriage that is surprising to many researchers is that married people report the highest rate of satisfaction in their intimate lives. Married persons reported feeling "loved," "wanted," and "belonging."[48]

23

Why are married people happier than divorced or single people?

Interestingly, the major factor for improved health and finances is that good marriages are emotionally fulfilling. The data correlates increases in marital happiness with improved physical health and longevity.[49] The exclusivity of monogamy fosters emotional stability. In addition, marriage and family satisfies one of mankind's deepest longings: to belong in a specific, intimate way to those who are "ours."

Whenever people have their deep human needs met, they are eager participants in the world around them; they contribute to the common good, which in turn builds up the whole of society. A healthy society responds by promoting and protecting marriage and family life so that the benefits rebound. Thus, married and communal life enhance each other, increasing the contentment of the married pairs.

Conversely, divorce doesn't usually solve a problem but creates new ones. A *USA Today* article details new research by University of Chicago sociologist Linda Waite. Waite found that in the most troubled marriages "about 80 percent were happy five years later."[50]

Waite's team discovered that the common assumption that unhappy couples are better off after a divorce is a myth. The study examined data from the National Survey of Family and Households. The research discovered that "on average unhappily married adults who divorced were no happier than unhappily married adults who stayed married when rated on any of twelve separate measures of psychological well-being," including depression and self-esteem.[51] Divorced people were not as happy as those who were married; they were much less happy.

24

Catholics oppose divorce on theological grounds, but isn't divorce better for all when there are problems in a marriage?

Divorce doesn't work as a means of solving the problems that caused the marriage to crumble. Divorced persons bring the same problems to a new marriage. Second and subsequent marriages are statistically more likely to end in divorce than first marriages.[52]

Seventy-six percent of second marriages break up within five years, as do 87 percent of third and 93 percent of fourth marriages—all of which expose the involved children to further turbulence and desertion.[53] Social science is quite clear: Marriage fosters health, happiness, wealth, and length of days to husband, wife, and children.

Surprisingly, a large majority of couples who contemplate divorce but stay together describe themselves as "happily married" five years later.[54] Staying together often works better than divorce.

25

What about children caught in unhappy marriages? Wouldn't they do better in a home free of marital strife?

Statistics do not support that myth. Even life in an "unhappy" marriage is generally better than growing up in a broken home. The '70s myth that "a happy divorce is better for children than an unhappy marriage" has been proven to be overwhelmingly false. Married parents who fight often have happier and healthier children than divorced parents.[55]

Children whose parents divorce are less educated, less successful in their adult careers, far more vulnerable to drugs and illegitimate pregnancy, and more prone to divorce themselves. Children of divorce are more likely to be injured accidentally than the children of intact marriages, and they die at a younger age.[56]

26

When parents remarry and establish "blended" families, doesn't that recapture the stable model of family life that children need after divorce?

Remarriage does not improve the lives of the children of divorce. Children in so-called "blended" families are dozens of times more likely to be the victims of physical violence or sexual abuse than children who live with both natural parents.[57] They are less healthy, happy, and successful in the long term.[58] Sadly, statistics show that revolving-door marriages expose children to further turbulence and desertion.[59] Social science statistics clearly indicate that the intact family, despite its challenges, is the better model for a healthy society.

27

If marriage and family life are the building blocks of society, why not expand the definition of family to include units established by same-sex couples?

Traditional models of marriage and family have proven effective for thousands of years. Traditional moral values for marriage and family are based on those objective realities of biology and sexual function plus the teachings found in the Bible concerning the relationship of man and woman.

Proposed new models of "marriage" are experimental and morally confused. Homosexual behavior is a serious disorder, a symptom of a deeper psychological conflict that has not been resolved.[60] Though many same-sex pairs are sincere in their desire to raise children, their lifestyle (and underlying struggles) is not a normal, healthy environment for children, who need both parents —male and female.

According to researchers, "the father and mother offer the child two different kinds of persons to learn about, as well as providing separate sources of love and support. . . . According to science, there are hundreds of nuances about men and women that even newborn infants can readily distinguish and that make a difference in the way the child develops. But aside from these developmental and psychological effects, there are also significant peripheral issues that come with same-sex parents that place additional risks upon children"[61] (see qq. 36, 94, 99).

28

Wouldn't public acceptance of homosexual unions and their families remove stigmas and create a condition of normality that would be healthy for the couple and their children?

A society may acknowledge some form of same-sex "marriage," but even legal sanction cannot make homosexual activity normal. Homosexual acts are intrinsically disordered.[62] The domestic life of homosexual pairs does not reflect the truth of male and female relationships and the bearing of children. Those relationships are inherently unstable. Youngsters raised in homes established by homosexual partners are at risk for multiple emotional disturbances, poor socialization, and violence. In addition, the risk of sexual abuse within the home is fifty times greater.[63]

29

If homosexual relationships are inherently unstable, isn't that due to a lack of a permanent bond? Wouldn't permission for them to marry solve the instability criticism?

The evidence argues against that assumption. In the Netherlands, where same-sex marriage has been legalized and no stigma constrains the relationship, the average length of a homosexual partnership is only a year and a half.[64] Homosexual pairs are free to establish permanent bonds without the permission or approval of societal institutions, but few have done so. The average length of a relationship in homosexual partners who describe themselves as "committed" is two to three years.[65] Homosexual partnerships are inherently unstable because of the unnatural purpose of the relationship. It is a myth that legalizing same-sex unions will stabilize the promiscuous lifestyle that is standard in homosexual pairs.

30

Isn't it prejudicial to label active homosexuals as "promiscuous"?

The word *promiscuous* has a specific meaning that is applied to an excessive behavior, whether homosexual or heterosexual. When the word is applied to heterosexual behavior, few claim that it is "prejudicial."

Research on the sexual habits of active homosexuals demonstrates the proclivity for multiple (often anonymous) partners. A San Francisco study illustrates the scope of the promiscuous pattern of sexual encounters for many homosexual people: 43 percent of males had had more than 500 sexual partners, and an astounding 79 percent were strangers. Only 3 percent had had fewer than ten sexual partners. Lesbians are less promiscuous than male homosexuals but more promiscuous than heterosexual women. [66]

Promiscuous patterns of this magnitude are best understood as a compulsive behavior. Dr. Richard P. Fitzgibbons found that "the sexually compulsive, highly reckless and life-threatening behavior in a large percentage of homosexuals would indicate the presence of an addictive disorder." Fitzgibbons notes that "this clinical view of much homosexual behavior as being addictive in nature is supported by numerous studies of the sexual practices of homosexuals and by the recent best estimates that one-half of the homosexual males in New York City are HIV positive." [67]

A more compassionate response by the medical community would be to acknowledge the addictive nature of homosexuality, and public policy guidelines would be set accordingly.

31

Could the specter of AIDS motivate same-sex pairs to practice monogamy? Wouldn't that benefit all of society by reducing the spread of the disease?

The fear of acquired immune deficiency syndrome (AIDS) apparently is not sufficient to motivate significant numbers of practicing homosexuals to abandon promiscuity. The Centers for Disease Control report that the average AIDS victim in the U.S. has had sixty sexual partners in the previous twelve-month period.[68] It cannot be assumed that all partners of the infected person were previously infected too or were told that the ill partner had AIDS.

One explanation for this reckless behavior is an addictive disorder that "resemble[s] substance abuse disorders in that individuals engage in compulsive behaviors that are medically hazardous. . . . The addictive nature of much of homosexual behavior explains why HIV [human immunodeficiency virus] infections have quadrupled in San Francisco since 1987."[69]

32

Wouldn't the short-term relationships characteristic of homosexual partners become monogamous as the pair adopted the standards of heterosexual marriages built on permanence and family?

The opposite effect is more likely. Heterosexual marriages will take on the attitude of "sexual pluralism" from the "marriage style" of homosexual pairs. Homosexual advocate Marvin Ellison has said as much: "Marriage should not be the exclusive signifier of family. . . . Society should follow the LGBT [lesbian, gay, bisexual, and transgendered] community and define partnerships and families functionally . . . urging more creative thinking about marriage . . . a greater openness to sexual pluralism."[70] He continues: "Heterosexual sex is no longer driven by procreative imperative. . . . To a considerable extent, the heterosexual culture is coming to resemble the gay culture with its 'notorious' gender flexibility openness to experimentation with diverse family forms."[71]

One widely circulated vision of homosexual "alliances" where parenthood and family are simulated includes this synthesis: "an alliance partaking equally of father-son, teacher-student, and big brother–little brother relationships . . . with the superadded bond of explicitly sexual love."[72]

Most active homosexuals view monogamy as undesirable or at least unachievable given the nature of the homosexual culture.[73] Many in the homosexual community actively resist "assimilation into the dominant heterosexual culture"[74] where homosexuals would be required to "deemphasize their difference from the cultural majority and present themselves as 'just like anybody else.'"[75]

33

Shouldn't we assume that there are fringe groups on both sides of the debate? Isn't it reasonable to say that some homosexual partners are committed and monogamous?

It is not reasonable because one cannot apply the standards of marriage to any homosexual partnership arrangement. Some homosexuals seek "marriage" as a badge of society's approval of their relationship. But securing a marriage license entails no monogamous requirement of the pair. They are free to live within the marriage as they prefer, assuming no laws are broken. Monogamy is not considered a benefit in most homosexual liaisons.

Robert P. George of Princeton University quotes from an essay called "Queer Liberalism?" in the June 2000 *American Political Science Review*. The article surveyed six books that explored same-sex marriage. George wrote, "None of the six authors affirmed sexual exclusivity as a precondition of same-sex marriage, and most rejected the idea that sexual fidelity should be expected of 'married' homosexual partners. For more than a decade, a wide array of authors who favor redefining marriage to include same-sex partners have advanced similar views. In a 1996 essay in the *Michigan Law Review*, University of Michigan law professor David Chambers even suggested that marriage should be redefined to include sexual unions of three or more people—so-called polyamorous relationships."[76]

Hence, promiscuity is a significant factor in homosexual relationships. A change in the law to accommodate some form of legal recognition will not solve the internal problems of a homosexual relationship. Children's best interests are not served in such relationships.

34

How can you discount the American Psychological Association's 2004 decision to endorse homosexual marriage?[77]

The American Psychological Association has a much-tarnished reputation. In 1999, the U.S. Congress censured the group for publishing dangerous suppositions. The House of Representatives passed a resolution "condemning and denouncing" the conclusions of an article in the association's *Psychological Bulletin* that suggested that pedophile relationships may not be dangerous and might be beneficial for "willing" children.[78]

Professional associations can do much good, but they also may become overly political. When homosexual activists seek positions of influence in any association for the purpose of politicizing the association's public stand in favor of homosexual goals, objectivity is lost (see qq. 35, 89, 90, 92). Hundreds of psychologists do not agree with the APA's position on the practice of homosexuality.[79]

35

What about the American Psychological Association's report that states there is "no evidence that lesbians and gay men are unfit to be parents"?[80]

That 1995 report also admits, "It should be acknowledged that research on lesbian and gay parents and their children is still very new and relatively scarce."[81] The author of that statement, Charlotte J. Patterson, is a lesbian activist. Patterson also admits to methodological flaws in the research, including lack of control groups and small samples. A professional review of the research data on homosexual parenting found that "the methods used in these studies are so flawed that the studies prove nothing. Therefore they should not be used in legal cases to make any argument about 'homosexual vs. heterosexual' parenting. Their claims have no basis."[82]

It is critical to dissect any data that make claims to prove that children from same-sex families are as safe and as well adjusted as the children raised in heterosexual families. There is no impartial, reliable data: No long-term studies that follow children into adulthood are available. Additionally, pediatricians have repeated a known truth: Children raised in traditional marriages have the substantial benefits of living with both mother and father.[83]

36

Have pediatricians issued a statement concerning children in same-sex partnerships?

Yes. The American College of Pediatricians statement is: "We expect societal forces to support the two-parent, father-mother family unit and provide for children role models of ethical character and responsible behavior."[84]

Specific to same-sex marriages, the group stated, "Same-gender 'marriage' is clearly a highly controversial cultural issue and represents a radical social experiment lacking unbiased research supporting its benefits. . . . Clearly, we are in a culture war for the life and health of families and their children."[85]

In some studies, children raised by homosexual parents appear to have sex-role confusion.[86] Studies have shown a high incidence of incest between minor children and homosexual parents of both sexes.[87]

37

There are respectable homosexually active men and women who are productive members of society with much to offer any child. Isn't it better for a child to be in such a home than to be raised in an orphanage? And what of lesbians who conceive and have their own child?

This question involves comparing the worst-case heterosexual home to a best-case same-sex partnership. Statistics underscore the dysfunctional relationship of most same-sex pairs (see qq. 29, 30, 92, 94). The percentage of healthy, stable, heterosexual couples is far greater than "stable" same-sex unions that are, by definition, not psychologically whole.

It is unfortunate when children are raised in orphanages, but it is not necessarily better to be adopted into a same-sex union.

Studies show that children raised in homes containing one biological parent are far more likely to be abused than in homes in which both biological parents reside.[88] Since two biological parents are not possible in a same-sex "marriage," and various other pathologies are common to homosexual partners, it would seem that a child is at less risk in a well-administered orphanage.

38

What about men breastfeeding? Haven't there been recent reports that it can be done? Wouldn't that prove men could be mothers?

There was a recent article exploring breastfeeding for men,[89] but the results for the few who have tried to induce lactation are questionable. The biological design of a mother and a father is irrefutable. Children need both, as *people* of the opposite gender, not only for milk.

39

Why does it matter whether or not there is a mother and father? Why wouldn't two devoted fathers or two loving mothers be as effective as one of each?

There are important childhood developmental stages that require both biological parents. The sexes are different. Men and women parent differently. Each bring different, complementary skills to childrearing. Men are more likely to play expansively with their children; women tend to be more practical. Mothers are generally more responsive to their child's immediate needs, while fathers tend to be more firm, more oriented to abstract standards of justice (right and wrong).[90] Mothers tend to emphasize emotional security, while fathers tend to stress competition and risk-taking. Mothers tend to seek the immediate well-being of the child, while fathers tend to foster long-term autonomy and independence.[91]

The presence of a dad is critical to a male child's learning—through interacting and observing with the father—the virtues of self-control, empathy, and appropriate male behavior, especially learning to respect women. Similarly, the presence of a father is vital for a female child's self-respect and eventual development of a healthy adult sexuality.[92] The presence of both parents is necessary for a well balanced emotional and mental development.

Our national epidemic of fatherlessness has spawned an epidemic of antisocial children. As one social scientist explained, a generation without fathers is a generation of fourteen-year-old boys with guns and fourteen-year-old girls with babies.[93] Children need both parents to learn all their life lessons well.

40

What disorders are borne by children in non-traditional families?

Children who are raised in "revolving door" homes (where adults come and go) experience disruption in emotional bonding, violation of trust, and exposure to all the personality defects that follow

rejection (perceived or actual). This is true in same-sex partnerships, divorce, stepfamilies, and single-parent heterosexual situations.[94] Among children aged twelve to seventeen, the number of
those suffering with depression, school behavioral problems, and
poor school performance was six times greater in children from
irregular family situations than those raised in married biological-
parent families.[95]

41

What about the example of children from non-traditional families in
Europe, where a more relaxed approach to sexuality accepts a broader
definition of family?

The social and economic costs are very high. Maggie Gallagher,
co-author of *The Case for Marriage*, notes that after forty years of
family diversity, Europe and America have not achieved greater
human happiness. She observed, "The consequence of our current retreat from marriage is not a flourishing libertarian social
order but a gigantic expansion of state power and a vast increase
in social disorder and human suffering."[96] Gallagher points out
that governments are left to shoulder the cost of massive social
needs left in the wake of shattered families: poverty, drug abuse,
unwed teen parents, health care, and school failures.[97]

  Gallagher offers a chilling prediction of what would happen if
a "unisex" version of marriage is sanctioned by the government:
"If the law embraces this message, it will become its carrier and
promoter. School textbooks, teen pregnancy programs, and abstinence programs will all be forced to carry this unisex marriage
vision. Religious people and social conservatives . . . unwilling
to champion this message will retreat from the public square. . . .
We do not know of any culture that has survived without a rea-
sonably functional marriage system. . . . A look at Europe does
not make one sanguine."[98]

42

For all the alarmist reports, isn't it realistic to expect that, after same-sex unions are part of the norm, society will settle down and go about business as usual?

Not at all. Where marriage is devalued, people no longer marry; they stop having children. Europeans marry less and cohabit more.

A more realistic appraisal requires society to admit that Europe is experiencing a "birth dearth"[99] that has brought catastrophic upheavals in immigration tensions, an aging population with heavy health care costs, and widespread anxiety over pension planning. Simply stated, Europe is not replacing itself. There are insufficient people to fill the jobs in many sectors, so large scale immigration is a necessary discomfort[100] if the nations are to maintain their economies.

Same-sex pairs are sterile. Gallagher concludes, "Marriage is not an option; it is a precondition for social survival. . . . It means losing limited government. . . . It means losing period."[101]

The Catholic Church has spoken frequently of a "culture of death" in which the contraceptive mentality, abortion, and high rates of divorce and homosexuality will bring about the inevitable population decline and loss of culture.[102]

43

Why can't Catholics see that any rejection of civil rights for homosexual people is pure bigotry? We no longer forbid interracial marriages. Why should such intolerance be tolerated?

There is no basis for the charge that Catholics are bigoted against homosexual persons. To disapprove of a proposed change in a norm of society is not the same as disapproving of the persons who make the proposal. Catholics defend the civil rights of all.[103] The charge of "bigotry" is a deflective tactic; it is intended to stop any discussion of the *facts* of homosexuality because the debate is re-centered on "bigotry."

Homosexual advocates have compared their push to legalize same-sex unions to the racial struggle for civil rights—with little success. People readily perceive that race is inherent, not chosen. Same-sex attraction is not chosen, but the homosexual lifestyle is a choice. Many black leaders have denounced the "gay-rights" movement's attempt to equate civil rights to "special rights" for homosexual partners.[104]

The debate is not about "rights," because homosexual persons *are* free to marry persons of the opposite sex. The difficulty is that they wish to redefine marriage (as if that were possible), an institution that predates any society, government, or political system. Homosexual activity is a choice one makes, a symptom of a psycho-social struggle, not a genetic condition (see q. 107). One is born into one's race or ethnic group, but no one is born to homosexuality; there is no genetic warrant to claim that anyone was "born that way" (see q. 108).

But there is justification for the claim that homosexual activists are intolerant of marriage as defined by five thousand years of human history and God's design for men and women.

44

Why do religious opponents of same-sex unions frame the debate as a conspiracy by homosexuals to affront God or abolish Judeo-Christian influence in society?

Religious opponents of same-sex unions frame the debate as one of urgent concern for all members of society, both those of a secular worldview and those of a biblically based worldview. We must live as an integrated society, which means that the laws will apply to all, regardless of religion or lack thereof. Our ability to establish public tranquillity will depend on establishing laws that foster the common good for the most people.

Catholics acknowledge that many persons, both secular and religious, do not understand the consequences that would follow legalization of same-sex unions. This lack of understanding is the result of a misplaced compassion for those with same-sex attraction and does not always constitute a malicious intent toward people of faith. But legalization of homosexual unions will have grave consequences for the whole of society, not only for those who are informed by the Judeo-Christian worldview. In other words, the consequences are neutral: All will suffer.

45

Isn't the entire debate about imposing one religious view on all the rest of the society?

That is an oversimplification that is quickly dispatched by reversing the question: "Isn't the entire debate about imposing homosexual ideas on all the rest of the society?"

Marriage must be defended by its traditional definition in order to have any meaning at all. Keep in mind that marriage as an *institution* is not exclusive. Members of both genders who are of legal age and unmarried are free to marry each other within the definition of marriage.

But the *definition* of marriage *is* exclusive in that it excludes marriage to multiple partners, children, siblings, etc. If the definition of marriage is reconfigured to mean a relationship with any being that one "loves," then marriage is reduced to a statement of sentiment. Logically, if same-sex pairs can be legalized as "married," why not threesomes or whatever configuration appeals to a petitioner for "marriage rights"?

To grasp the importance of maintaining the traditional definition of marriage, consider a society where homosexual pairs are the dominant marriage arrangement. How would a society function in which the fundamental arrangement of people is by gender rather than the integration of both genders? How long could such a society exist? It can be seen very quickly that no nation can exist without traditional marriages engaged in reproduction and education of the young. Yet nations can and have existed for millennia *without* same-sex unions.

This is because the template for marriage is written in both the human heart and in biology. Marriage reflects the complementarity of the male and the female. It is this reality that inspires cultures and governments to structure laws and public policy to support traditional families. Couples inherently understand that their personal commitment is also a commitment that benefits the whole of society.

The reality of complementarity, in both heart and biology, serves the whole of mankind. It acknowledges a two-gendered world in which each gender has specific attributes—beyond mere body parts—that are necessary to build a healthy, integrated society.

Seen from this perspective, it is clear that it is those who advocate for same-sex marriage who are attempting to impose their definition of marriage on the rest of society, and not the other way around.

2

The Nature of Marriage

46

What is so definite about marriage that it is not open to redefinition?

Marriage has definite parameters because it contains specific elements ordered to a specific purpose: the permanent, exclusive, covenantal bond of one man and one woman ordered to the unity of the couple and to the children their love may bring forth. If new elements are introduced in an attempt to redefine marriage, then the elements of male and female, exclusivity, permanence, and unity are violated. Minus those elements, it is no longer marriage but simply cohabitation. These elements are based on both biology and biblical revelation: "Male and female he created them" (Gen. 1:27).

47

Physiology may dictate one form of sexual intimacy, but homosexual pairs have found alternate uses of the sexual design to be satisfactory. Why isn't their sexual expression equally as valid as heterosexual intercourse?

Homogenital acts may bring temporary satisfaction, but they result in long-term grief, both physically and emotionally. Such acts, a parody of the real meaning of sexual intimacy, do not reflect the given truth of human sexual design and function. The constant misuse of the person and the body destroys health and psychological equilibrium.

48

To describe a homosexual relationship as a parody of real sexual intimacy is a bigoted view. Wouldn't you agree?

No. Bigoted means a prejudice that is unfounded in fact. Homosexual acts are not true sexual acts. True sexual intercourse gathers the opposite halves of the human species into a marital embrace that constitutes a re-union of all that is human into one flesh. Only the marital embrace of husband and wife is ordered toward a fruitful manifestation of their love: a new human being.

Homosexual acts are intrinsically sterile.

A homosexual act attempts to join what is unjoinable in any sense of completeness. Russian philosopher Nicholas Berdyaev explained the need for sexual complementarity by observing that loneliness is part of the human condition; loneliness is the realization that, deep down, neither a man alone nor a woman alone is complete. Each lacks the perfection and capabilities of the opposite sex, and in that sense each is incomplete—and lonely— without the other.[1]

A homosexual act is incomplete because it literally lacks the "other half." Incompleteness leads to dissatisfaction, a "something is missing" lassitude that overwhelms a person whenever a relationship fails to reflect an authentic meaning and purpose. Dissatisfaction drives participants to seek novel or even extreme measures to generate new excitement that will cover—only temporarily—the realization that "something is missing."

49

Why must the "other half" of a marriage be of the opposite sex?

The first argument for opposites as the only authentic bond is from biology. Nature's clear design intended male and female to "fit together."

This fitting together is productive, as the internal physiology responds to the external design, so that the generative donation of the male (husband) is received and nurtured by the female (wife). Through this unity of the human species, they conceive a new person.

Thus, the deepest unity a man or a woman can experience with another human person is the authentic joining of the two opposites to become one whole—the male and female are different biologically *and* emotionally. The fullest experience of being human is found in giving oneself to the "other," being received, and then receiving the gift of self in return. This mutuality integrates the two halves of the human existence, the male and the female. Pope John Paul II refers to this as "original unity," and it is "precisely masculinity and femininity that allow this unity."[2]

In natural law—observable by natural reason without aid of divine revelation—Aristotle noted: "Cohabitation among human kind is not for the mere raising of children but also for the purposes of a partnership in life: for from the first the offices of man and woman are distinct and different; thus they mutually supply for one another, putting their several advantages into the common stock."[3]

Marriage is understood in both the natural law and in divine law as ordered to one man and one woman and the children that are the fruit of their union. Same-sex unions are a distortion of marriage.

50

If procreation is a necessary element of marriage, what about infertile couples? Is their marriage invalid?

No. The marriage of an infertile couple is as equally valid as a couple who is fertile. Infertile couples are not frustrating the procreative purpose of nature or the biological design of the body. A true unity of male and female characterizes their intimacy. They are partners for the challenge and adventure of life. As Scripture says, "It is not good that the man should be alone; I will make him a helper fit for him" (Gen. 2:18).

Couples who discover that they are sterile often suffer greatly.[4] Many of them desire children. There are children who, due to tragic circumstances, need a safe and loving home. Thus, adoption is a revered element of the charitable mission of the Church.

51

If the Catholic Church places a premium on married couples having children, why does the Church forbid in-vitro fertilization?

The Catholic Church shares the profound disappointment of couples who desire a child but have not conceived, but it prohibits fertilization that takes place *outside* of the sexual act, because it deprives marital union of its inherent meaning.[5] It is permissible for doctors to facilitate conception by making it more likely to occur by natural means.[6]

This circumstance serves to illustrate a moral truth: It is not permissible to commit an illicit act in order to achieve a good intention. The principle is grasped easily if applied to support for one's family: Economic support is a good intention, but theft, prostitution, or smuggling illegal substances in order to provide that support is not permissible. Most fertilization technologies create "surplus" embryos that are discarded. The process treats new life as if it were a product to be used or discarded at the discretion of doctors and parents.

52

Could it be that Catholics simply have an anti-sex attitude? Isn't the Catholic Church prudish and unenlightened about most aspects of sexuality?

A glance through the writings of John Paul II on sexuality[7] will quickly dispel any such thought. The Church believes and teaches that marital sex is holy (see qq. 72, 73). The Church teaches that the material world is good because God created it. The human body, male and female, is "very good" (Gen. 1:31). The Church further extends its teaching that the body is good, because it will be resurrected in Christ. Since God instituted marriage and made a body for man and woman that is "good" and united them as "one flesh," the Church teaches that the body must be treated properly and that the sexual union of a husband and wife is sacred.

The body is not separate from the person. The person manifests actions and free will through the body.[8] Misuse of the sexual faculties is misuse of the person, body and soul. A person may never be used, or consent to be used, as an object of desire rather than as a whole person with an eternal destiny. It is only in the marriage covenant that the whole person is respected for the entirety of his being, including his "otherness," not simply as a tool for sexual gratification.

The Church never wearies of defending marriage as the proper and only authentic setting for sexual intimacy. Because the conjugal act is a gift of the whole self, it is protected within the heart of an exclusive, permanent bond so that the whole person may develop and grow in the confidence of the lifetime commitment that each has made to the other.

53

If marriage is all that its advocates claim, why is the divorce rate so high? Perhaps same-sex pairs would reinvigorate the institution of marriage.

Same-sex partnerships would not give marriage a new lift; it would further erode marriage as an institution (see q. 16).

The double tragedy of divorce is the loss of respect for the institution of marriage and the personal unhappiness of the divorced couple. Our public policy of "no-fault divorce" and the weakening of social pressures have made it easier for troubled couples to divorce. This has proven tragic for the health and well being of families. Social scientists tracked a sharp rise in the divorce statistics in the later half of the twentieth century[9] due to the "sexual revolution" that began in the 1960s. Fractured families soon followed; this led in turn to a new generation of people who are wary of marriage and unsure of the true meaning and purpose of marriage.

54

Why did the "sexual revolution" lead to divorce rather than more "sexy" marriages?

Some people did expect "sexual liberation" to add sizzle and spice to Ozzie and Harriet's lives. What it brought was a loss of respect for both marriage and sex. What went wrong? The answer is partly philosophical and partly natural.

Philosophically, Western societies substituted scientific primacy for Judeo-Christian morality.[10] It is a utopian urge that seeks to perfect man via science and technology. Distilled, the concept means that when/if everyone's material needs are met and each person orders his life as freely as possible according to his own disposition, then man will be "naturally" good. Yet, "naturally" he is not. Science has yet to locate the center of pride, greed, envy, revenge, or selfishness, much less propose antidotes.

Furthermore, the Judeo-Christian worldview regards science as God's own creation—it is the *misuse* of science for ideological purposes that people of faith object to. Thus, to ignore the science of biology and physiology in order to bend nature to serve a "sexual revolution" against nature, including the homosexual agenda, is hardly "scientific."

55

Where has science as ideology had an impact on marriage?

Psychologist B. F. Skinner's 1948 novel *Walden Two* welcomed the "weakening of the family structure [that] will make experimental breeding possible."[11] Soon science offered commercially available anovulants. Couples were free to limit their families without limiting marital intimacy. Limited births, in theory, meant fewer families needed public assistance.

But marriages fell apart in the wake of the pill and no-fault divorce. The utopian promise failed modern man, but marriages were blamed. The consequences: Divorce rates doubled within a decade.

56

What does "the pill" have to do with divorce?

The pill and other contraceptive means do not "liberate" the couple as supposed. Instead, contraceptives create a sex-on-demand attitude within the marriage. When the procreative power is divorced from the marital embrace, the spouses become little more than objects to be used for personal gratification (see qq. 60, 61). Pope Paul VI wrote one of the most poignant and prophetic lines ever written about the consequences of contraceptive sex: Man "may forget the reverence due to a woman" and "reduce her to being a mere instrument for the satisfaction of his own desires, no longer considering her his partner whom he should surround with care and affection."[12] Note that his comment was not a "religious rant" or "biblical fundamentalism" but a simple statement of cause and effect beyond any religious context.

Couples who follow the natural fertility cycles of the wife and avoid chemical or mechanical means of birth control have the lowest divorce rate—under 3 percent.[13] Couples who use natural means of fertility regulation report that periods of abstinence are a reminder of the power of their love. Plus, it creates a monthly honeymoon-like reunion.[14]

57

Birth control is birth control, whether "natural" or mechanical; the intent is the same. Why do Catholics teach that "natural family planning" is morally superior when it is simply a primitive means of contraception?

Natural family planning can never be compared to contraception, primitive or otherwise. Contraception thwarts the natural end of the marital act in a variety of unsafe and immoral ways. NFP, when used to space children, abstains from the marital act during the woman's fertile period, which is neither unsafe nor immoral when done for just reasons.

It is a common misconception that natural methods of fertility regulation are no more or less moral than mechanical or chemical means of regulation. While it is true that in both instances the intent is to prevent conception, all methods are not morally licit. The natural cycle of feminine fertility provides infertile periods. It can be licit to cooperate with this cyclical timing in order to postpone births. (See appendix II for a listing of NFP resources.)

Couples who cooperate with God's design do not obstruct the totality, the fullness, of the conjugal act. The Catholic Church teaches that an unnatural obstruction violates the unity of the conjugal purpose; such acts are intrinsically evil.[15] NFP preserves the integrity of the marital union in all its dimensions. Periodic abstinence spaces births but insures that each time the couple comes together, they bring the fullness of their being, not a truncated half version of the union.

Using NFP for "just reasons"[16] is a licit means of family planning. Mechanical and chemical contraception in essence divides and tears asunder the inseparable purposes of marital union: unity of the pair (husband and wife) and procreation. It is a divorce of the purposes of the marital embrace that too often leads to a divorce of the couple.

Contraceptive sex deliberately casts aside God's dual purposes for sexual expression. It is a rebellion against God's gift, accepting one part of the gift but rejecting the other. Natural regulation preserves the complete gift; it does not take the pleasure and reject the life-giving power of the act. Contraception aims at the very core of human existence. A contraceptive mentality is at the root of what has been called the "culture of death." [17]

58

Isn't it theological doublespeak to refer to "just reasons" for using Catholic family planning techniques? Who decides what the "just reasons" are?

The husband and wife decide. It is not duplicitous for the Church to encourage couples to both be generous toward life and practice responsible parenthood. [18] Each family may determine when their circumstances (health, economics) indicate that spacing of children is a responsible decision.

59

What about the claim that the Catholic Church simply wants to insure that Catholics are numerous, and therefore Catholics are forbidden to use birth control?

All Christians should understand that sex is part of God's design to increase his own family for all eternity. [19] It is not a "Catholic" only command but the first command from God to man: "Be fruitful and multiply" (Gen. 1:28). Each new baby is more than another body on this earth. The new child is also a person with an eternal destiny, an ultimate purpose beyond this earthly life.

Recognizing that all creation is from God and belongs to God is a fundamental way of understanding our existence. Many couples—not Catholics only—have come to view their sexuality as Trinitarian—that is, as the husband, the wife, and God. Couples who cherish their marriage as a sacramental vocation must be open to new life. Couples who are properly ordered toward life do not use NFP indiscriminately. The time and circumstances that might lead a couple to space births are a matter of individual conscience.

60

If science makes sex without babies possible, why is that so wrong?

God joined the unitive significance (love-giving) and procreative significance (life-giving) of the conjugal embrace in one act. To separate the two with contraceptive devices is "to make (re-create, re-make) human sexuality other than what it is and what it is for. Metaphysically, this is an unreal attempt to fashion a reality of our own, and, morally it is not just dangerous but damaging."[20] And the statistics attest to just how damaging re-creating sexual morality has been for society.

There is a lost dimension in contraceptive sex; "love making" is trivialized once it is stripped of its essential property to bring forth fruit born of that love. In John Paul II's terminology, people who contracept "tell a lie with their bodies," because their bodies speak a language of total, unconditional, and permanent self-donation when, in fact, they are doing nothing of the sort.[21] The divorce rate for contracepting couples is nearly 50 percent.[22]

61

Blaming the divorce rate on contraception is a stretch, isn't it?

Easy contraceptives had a domino effect. Wide use of contraceptives also paved the way for easy adultery. With millions of women "on the pill," fear of pregnancy as a result of illicit sex diminished, and adultery increased. The "swinging sixties" was not kind to marriages. Mohandas Gandhi had a prescient vision: "Any large use of the [contraceptive] methods is likely to result in the dissolution of the marriage and in free love."[23]

Objectively, contraception severs the profound link between sex and marriage; as such it is distinctly anti-marital. Theologically, couples are not open to "share in the creative power and fatherhood of God." [24] Once one has turned aside God's procreative plan, it is a short step from there to turning from God's plan for the permanency of marriage.

62

Why does permanence matter more than love? There are weddings in which the couple's promise is "as long as we both shall love."

The promise of permanence is love—real love, not just sentimental emotion. It's easy to be "in love" and romantic when all goes well. When illness or financial strain and the inevitable disappointments of life bump against sentimental "love," that love is lost. Permanence fosters security in the relationship between spouses. Security engenders the trust that is crucial to genuine intimacy.

Marriage is designed to be permanent; it is the union of two lives and their commitment to the children who are the fruit of that union. When sex is emptied of procreative power, sex is devalued to little or no meaning beyond a momentary pleasure, and *permanence* is no longer necessary.

Thus, sex is cut off from the realm of the holy, life-giving gift of one's self. This violent severance of union and procreation has wreaked violence on the whole of the society. Sex, no longer holy, is relegated instead to an instrument of a "use and be used" culture of nihilistic hedonism. That hedonism has carried us beyond the casual acceptance of contraception, to divorce, and now to proposals for same-sex "marriages."

As one bishop explained, "The union of the couple in turn becomes a selfish encounter of exploitation of the other. Since unions are then selfish encounters of exploitation, the sexual identity of the partners no longer becomes important, and society is in the situation that it is now, where same-sex marriages are allowed by law and civil unions are being proposed as the norm. . . . Our society is sick because we have sinned against the truth."[25]

63

Opposition to contraceptives is precisely what some characterize as unenlightened about the Catholic Church's stance on sexual morality. Weren't social factors, and not "the pill," to blame for the rise in divorce rates?

Use of contraception *is* a social factor. Millions have defaced their bodies by sterilization. Contraception is a barometer of the cultural mind-set. It is part of the science-as-savior mentality that rejects traditional morality in favor of a new morality based on how-many-consequences-can-science-erase when people violate the old morality. The idea is that any immoral act is transformed into a moral act by the elimination of the consequences. Such clouded thinking only delays the inevitable damage that is borne by the whole of society.

If the Church was "unenlightened" on the matter, so was the culture at large. It should be recalled that prior to 1930, the ban on contraception was all but universal in church *and* state. It was illegal to sell or send contraceptives through the U.S. Post Office.[26]

There was a cultural consensus that use of contraceptives was a depraved—hardly enlightened—act. It was understood that such acts were a blow to families, the root of society.

To illustrate the magnitude of the decision by the Anglican church's 1930 Lambeth Conference to approve limited use of contraceptives, consider this statement by a stunned *Washington Post*: "Carried to its logical conclusion, the committee's report, if carried into effect, would sound the death knell of marriage as a holy institution by establishing degrading practices that would encourage indiscriminate immorality. The suggestion that the use of legalized contraception would be 'careful and restrained' is preposterous."[27]

Far from unenlightened on the matter of contraception, the Catholic Church saw herself "standing erect in the midst of the moral ruin that surrounds her, in order that she may preserve the chastity of the nuptial union from being defiled by this foul stain, raises her voice in token of her divine ambassadorship and through our mouth proclaims anew: any use whatsoever of matrimony exercised in such a way that the act is deliberately frustrated in its natural power to generate life is an offense against the law of God and nature, and those who indulge in it are branded with the guilt of grave sin."[28]

64

Why doesn't the Catholic Church recognize the freedom of couples to determine the size of their families?

The Church does recognize that freedom, and it urges couples to use this freedom with wisdom and maturity. A mature understanding of sexual freedom within marriage treats sex as sacred precisely because of the spiritual dimension of the procreative powers. Fr. John Hardon wrote very cogently on sex and sanctity: "But no believer in Christ can become holy unless the sexual desires in his or her life are in harmony with the will of God. . . . They love God more than themselves."[29] When one does not exercise control, sex controls the person. Sex separated from the divine love of God too frequently becomes lust. Lust is destructive of the inner life and often has tragic consequences for the marriage.

A generous spirit toward children is a grace and a virtue. Each couple decides how best to space their children in their particular circumstances (medical, educational, financial). At times, this generous spirit is sacrificial.

The Catholic model for conjugal chastity is difficult to hear with ears accustomed to Madison Avenue's song of love, but many couples who have learned to follow God's plan testify to the wonders of a holy and sanctified married love.

65

Why not accept contraception as a necessary part of modern sexuality?

The question obscures the cost of contraception—not only in failed marriages but in costs to the woman who uses the pill as her method of choice. The use of anovulants "can cause breast cancer, blood clotting, and liver tumors among younger women. Fatal heart attacks are approximately twice as frequent among women who take the pill."[30] Reduced fertility when a woman does wish to conceive is an additional risk.

Others costs of today's "modern sexuality" based on a contraceptive mentality are increased promiscuity and sexually transmitted diseases. Promiscuity (fornication and adultery) operates in a new-found freedom from fear of unplanned pregnancy. Premarital sex is now a common feature of dating—although in most cases it is not strictly premarital since no marriage follows. The norm for "moral" people in many societies is several serial relationships before marriage and casual, recreational "hooking-up" for amoral people.

Predictably, rates of sexually transmitted diseases have skyrocketed. Added to the statistics on casual promiscuity is the rampant increase in abortions due to contraception failures. Even women who are "pro-choice" should know that abortion violates a woman's body and has serious long-term health consequences.[31] Thirty years ago people were either married or single.[32] Today, contraception makes serial cohabitation a "lifestyle choice," even though studies prove that the best sex is married sex.[33]

Furthermore, the health benefits of marriage (see qq. 1, 21, 22) are not found in couples who merely cohabit.[34]

66

Why do so many couples choose cohabitation rather than marriage?

For most couples it is fear of failure and a misunderstanding of what marriage truly means. Many are themselves the products of "no-fault" divorces that began in the 1970s. No-fault laws permitted some couples to escape disastrous situations, but in the wake of the "swinging sixties" it encouraged millions of couples to abandon merely "ordinary" marriages and search for an illusive "perfect" happiness.

One reason given for the fear of marriage is: "The bad marriage haunts us in part because we have reduced the marriage commitment to a single, grim, frightening phrase: Couples should 'stay together for the sake of the children.' The vision it conjures—of loveless, bitter, tight-lipped martyrs living in hell with their equally miserable kids—is impossible to uphold as a moral ideal."[35]

Meanwhile, despite contraception and abortion, the illegitimacy rate has increased 66 percent since 1980.[36] Those numbers may indeed indicate that despite fear of marriage, the natural human urge to have a family prevails, however misshapen the *form* of family may be (see q. 37).

67

Sex is a natural human drive. Marriage does not work out for everyone, but Catholics expect all unmarried people, homosexual and heterosexual, to be celibate?

Yes. Sex is reserved for married people because sex makes babies and babies need mothers and fathers in a permanent, committed bond.

Chastity is a gift too, though. As the *Catechism* says, "Chastity includes an apprenticeship in self-mastery, which is a training in human freedom. The alternative is clear: either man governs his passions and finds peace, or he lets himself be dominated by them and becomes unhappy."[37] While sex is a natural drive, it is not like thirst or hunger. A sexual relationship is not the validation of a person's life, as Hollywood so often portrays. A productive, active single life is rewarding.

Single people are called to chastity—they are simply faithful in advance to the one they will eventually marry. Or if called to the single life, theirs is a witness to self-mastery. The *Catechism* points out that "homosexual persons are called to chastity. By the virtues of self-mastery that teach them inner freedom, at times by the support of disinterested friendship, by prayer and sacramental grace, they can and should gradually and resolutely approach Christian perfection."[38]

68

What is the moral ideal for marriage?

One man, one woman, in an exclusive, permanent bond that is open to the gift of children. This ideal satisfies human biology and emotional needs while providing society with the primary unit of the community—the family.

69

Not all marriages are made in heaven. What about bad marriages?

Some marriages are simply lackluster; they are in need of redoubled effort to cultivate the virtues both persons originally found pleasing in the other. This is hard work—it requires prayer and grace—but it preserves the couple and is profoundly better for children than a divorce that sunders the family.

Where a marriage has serious fissures, pastoral and professional counseling is a wise course. In extreme cases (physical abuse, persistent infidelities) canon law provides legal separation without dissolving the marriage.[39] This can seem harsh, but the Church has no authority to dissolve the bond of a licit marriage,[40] as Jesus himself warned, "What therefore God has joined together, let not man put asunder" (Matt. 19:6).

Such situations are sad indeed and require sacrificial courage and perseverance in prayerful expectation that the difficulties may eventually be resolved.[41]

3

What Does the Church Teach?

70

Does the Catholic Church have an understanding of marriage beyond making babies and "until death do us part"?

The common misunderstanding is that the Catholic Church has a myopic, one-dimensional view of marriage. The truth is that the Church has a wealth of insight on marriage. The distinctive feature of Catholic teaching is respect for the whole person, eschewing a false division of body and spirit. Thus, the union of husband and wife is both unitive and procreative[1] (see q. 49).

71

Why do Catholics make a distinction between contraception and natural methods of regulating fertility? Isn't it hypocritical since the goal is the same and only the technology is different?

The Church urges couples to reflect upon the necessity to maintain the inseparable nature of marriage, the unitive and procreative. Jesus said, "What God has joined together, let no man separate" (Mark 10:8–9). Most often this command is thought to apply to marriage and divorce, but it also applies to the dual purpose of marriage. God is the Master of life, but couples reject God's design when they reject their fertility while keeping the gift of sex. In effect, they say to God, "You are the Lord of my life, but not my fertility." God joined the unitive and procreative meaning and purpose of the marital embrace; no man should separate them one from the other.

72

Why is the Catholic Church so protective of marriage?

Marriage is not just any association between persons; it was established by God to have its own nature, essential properties, and purpose.[2] No ideology or political system "can erase from the human spirit the certainty that marriage exists solely between a man and a woman . . . proper and exclusive to themselves. . . . In this way they mutually perfect each other, in order to cooperate with God in the procreation and upbringing of new human lives."[3]

Man, in the image of God, was created male and female, as equal and complementary to one another. Sexuality, thus, is integral to the whole person, body and spirit.[4] Marriage is that "form of life that is a communion of persons . . . involving the use of the sexual faculty."[5] To assist the Creator with bringing forth the family of God, "in the Creator's plan, sexual complementarity and fruitfulness belong to the very nature of marriage."[6] On the mystical level, the marriage of man and woman is an "efficacious sign of the covenant between Christ and the Church (Eph. 5:32)."[7]

73

How can the marriage of a man and a woman be a sign of Christ and the Church?

As one U.S. bishop wrote, "From the first page to the last, the Bible is a love story. It begins in Genesis with the marriage of Adam and Eve, and it ends in the book of Revelation with the wedding feast of the Lamb—the marriage of Christ and his Bride, the Church."[8]

The Bible frequently compares the relationship between husband and wife to that between God and Israel (cf. Hos. 9:1) and between Christ and his Church (cf. Eph. 5:21−32). Consequently, the Church views infidelity and other disordered forms of sexual expression as comparable to idolatry or blasphemy.

The Church considers the marital union of husband and wife to be an icon, an image of the life-giving love that flows between the three Persons of the Holy Trinity. For Catholics, marriage is a holy, life-giving vocation. It is analogous to the vocation of the priesthood, which is the conduit of divine life.

Thus, in the mystical vision, the Church as Bride and Christ as Bridegroom give to each other. The Bridegroom, Christ, pours out his divine life for his beloved. The Bride, the Church, receives his love, nurtures his children with the sacraments, and gives back to her Bridegroom the family of God, the immortal souls who live forever in eternity.

74

Does the Catholic Church expect to prohibit same-sex marriage for non-Catholics?

Yes, the Church hopes to assist all people of good will to learn the fundamental truths of man, woman, and marriage.

The Church also has an identity as a tiny nation; under the title of the Holy See, the Vatican city-state is a member of the world's community of nations. As an independent nation, the Holy See also participates at the United Nations. Its diplomatic corps is actively engaged in promoting a "culture of life" throughout the world. The Church seeks public policies that benefit all societies and each individual.

The Church bears a prophetic witness to the world regarding the consequences of violating God's design and purpose. It teaches that there are "absolutely no grounds for considering homosexual unions to be in any way similar or even remotely analogous to God's plan for marriage and family. . . . Under no circumstances can they be approved."[9]

75

Has the Church always opposed homosexual unions?

Yes. All consensual homosexual acts, in any context, are "intrinsically disordered."[10] No "commitment" or legal sanction can justify an intrinsically immoral act. The constant Judeo-Christian witness, based in Scripture, has been to prohibit homosexual acts (see appendix I).

The early Church Fathers taught against all manner of sin, including any form of homosexual activity. A few examples suffice to illustrate the consistent witness:

- "You shall not commit pederasty."[11]

- "Having become effeminate among the Greeks, and a teacher of the disease of effeminacy to the rest of the Scythians."[12]

- "Men are emasculated, and all the pride and vigor of their sex is effeminated in the disgrace of their enervated body."[13]

It should be noted that homosexual practices in the ancient world most often accompanied the depravities of paganism and idolatry. St. John Chrysostom wrote, "[The pagans] were addicted to the love of boys . . . and they had houses for this purpose in which it was openly practiced. And if all that was done among them was related, it would be seen that they openly outraged nature, and there was none to restrain them. . . . As for their passion for boys, whom they called their *paedica*, it is not fit to be named."[14]

76

If the Catholic Church does not approve of homosexual marriages for its members, does it at least counsel civil tolerance for homosexual unions?

No. While care must be taken to avoid unjust discrimination, the Church forbids cooperation with laws that permit same-sex unions.[15] The Church teaches that "civil law cannot contradict right reason without losing its binding force on conscience."[16] The Church forbids all consensual homosexual acts because Scripture condemns all homosexual acts (see appendix I). Such acts are not to be accepted for any reason or purpose, even where legalized.[17]

It is critical to note that the Church also counsels citizens that "approval or legalization of evil is something far different from toleration of evil."[18] The Church does not permit believers to cooperate with political measures that would legalize "specific rights for cohabiting homosexual persons."[19]

In civil matters, including the formulation of public policy, the Church stresses that the whole truth must be considered: Homosexual persons may not be unjustly discriminated against with respect to universal rights enjoyed by all persons; but at the same time, citizens must remind governments to contain the phenomenon of homosexual unions so as to "safeguard public morality" and avoid "exposing young people to erroneous ideas about sexuality and marriage."[20]

77

What does the Church expect of its members in those societies where same-sex unions have already been legalized?

The Catholic Church considers all laws legalizing same-sex unions as "gravely unjust."[21] Where same-sex unions are legal, every Catholic has the *duty* to give "clear and emphatic opposition." Furthermore, each Catholic "must refrain from any kind of formal cooperation in the enactment or application of such gravely unjust laws. . . . In this area, everyone can exercise the right of conscientious objection."[22]

78

How emphatic must Catholic opposition to legalized same-sex unions be?

"Emphatic" may not be construed as passive acceptance of a policy. As with abortion, Catholics have a serious moral obligation to object to the legalization of same-sex unions and voice disapproval when homosexual pairs are portrayed as "married" in entertainment or art. Catholics must insist that political representatives rescind policies and laws that support same-sex unions. Catholic parents should protect their children from schools and programs in which same-sex unions are presented as a normal lifestyle.

Catholics must refuse to implement or apply policies that accommodate or promote same-sex unions. For example, advertisers may not design advertising that portrays same-sex pairs as married, nor may teachers instruct students that same-sex unions are viable as an "alternate lifestyle." In some cases, "emphatic" resistance may bring economic or social hardship. Despite that possibility, Catholics may not cooperate with evil and are called in charity to endure hardships for the sake of the gospel.

79

May Catholics vote for politicians who support same-sex unions?

No. A Catholic lawmaker is forbidden to vote for a law that institutes same-sex unions. Because it is wrong to vote for such a measure, it is also wrong to vote for a politician who would pass such a law.[23] In a situation in which all candidates in a field in both parties have declared support for same-sex unions, Catholics should vote in a way that would cause the least amount of damage.

80

What must a Catholic politician do when laws are proposed to legalize same-sex unions?

The Church teaches that "when legislation in favor of the recognition of homosexual unions is proposed for the first time in a legislative assembly, the Catholic lawmaker has a moral duty to express his opposition clearly and publicly and to vote against it. To vote in favor of a law so harmful to the common good is gravely immoral."[24] In summary: A Catholic politician who publicly supports same-sex unions or same-sex marriages commits a gravely immoral offense against God. If a Catholic politician does not make his opposition to same-sex unions known publicly (apart from very special circumstances[25]), that failure to speak out is gravely immoral. No politician as a matter of principle may support these policies.

81

Isn't the view of the Catholic Church toward homosexual persons negative?

No, the Church sees all persons as made in the image of God. The Church calls each human to the fullness of being in God's image. Homosexual persons are due respect and just treatment.[26] While homosexual *acts* are always gravely immoral,[27] the Church makes a clear distinction between the act and the orientation.[28] It is not a sin to struggle with homosexual orientation. Only the act (or use of material depicting the act) is immoral.

82

May a Catholic with homosexual orientation live and work in a setting in which active homosexuality is present as long as he is chaste?

A homosexual person living a life of chastity should not live and work in an environment in which homosexual practice is present. All Catholics must "avoid the near occasion of sin" wherever the setting constitutes a temptation to sin. For example, an alcoholic should not seek employment as a wine merchant. The virtue of prudence instructs all persons to avoid situations in which one's resolve to avoid sin is subject to consistent temptation.

Homosexual persons are encouraged to seek healthy friendships with persons of both sexes. Participation in social, educational, and sporting events as well as numerous other settings may offer homosexual persons a full, but chaste, social life with both sexes. Fr. John Harvey, founder of Courage,[29] an international spiritual support organization for homosexual persons who seek to live a chaste life, writes, "One of the goals of Courage is to form chaste friendships with persons of the other sex and well as persons of one's own sex."[30] Healthy, supportive social interaction with both sexes opens new insights into both genders.

4

What Does Medical Science Say?

83

Aren't there new studies that challenge old assumptions about gender?

Yes, there are radical challenges to the standard use of the term *gender* that have enormous political consequences. A "gender perspective" has already been mainstreamed in education and international governmental agencies.

A book entitled *The Gender Agenda* details how and why gender has been hijacked from biology and forced to serve as a soldier in an ideological war. Its author, Dale O'Leary, observed, "The gender agenda begins with a false premise—that the differences between men and women are social constructs. . . . All differences between men's and women's activities and achievements are artificial, [so] they can and should be eliminated."[1]

Some definitions from the *Oxford Dictionary*[2] aid clarity: Sex is defined as "each of the main groups (male or female) into which living things are categorized on the basis of their reproductive functions," and gender is "a person's sex." The move to use *gender* rather than *sex* on forms and in policy planning—even laws —is an attempt to invalidate the biological truth of a person's sex and to give favor to how one understands oneself.

84

How does the definition of gender affect the question of marriage?

The radical theory insists that the term *gender* is a learned construct: Roles such as father, mother, husband, and wife are not *biologically* based but socially imposed. If gender roles are constructs, then they also must be flexible enough to permit a man to reconstruct his "gender" (though not his biology) and identify his role or himself as "woman" or for a woman to act in the male role of father/husband if she chooses.

A recent Vatican document that addresses current gender questions warns that these theories "call into question the family, in its natural two-parent structure of mother and father, and make homosexuality and heterosexuality virtually equivalent, in a new model of polymorphous sexuality."[3]

85

Is how we think about gender so important? Isn't it okay for a man to be a stay-at-home dad or the wife to be the primary financial support of a family?

The question is far deeper than who stays home and who goes to work. These choices are recent options. Only a hundred years ago most fathers were at home, because work was at home (farm, shop, etc.).

Advocates of same-sex unions deny the significance of the biological differentiation in human beings. "If the differentiation between male and female is insignificant, then the sexual relationship between a man and a woman cannot be significantly different than the sexual relationship between two men or two women. And if that is true, it then becomes impossible to see how sexual activity is linked to marriage."[4]

Gender adjusters propose that the genders are interchangeable, that the gender-specific roles of husband and wife and father and mother are not intrinsic to biology, and thus a woman could be the "husband" of another woman, or a man could be the "mother" of a child. To reject the reality of one's gender-specific identity is in itself a willful rebellion against observable order and is indicative of a psychological deficit.

86

Some persons are more comfortable functioning as the other gender. What's wrong with that?

True, some persons are suffering from gender-identity disorder. Again, it is indicative of a serious psychological problem. Proper sex identity is a developmental task that occurs between the ages of two and four years.

Just as there is an optimum time to learn how to walk, there is an optimum time to learn one's sex. When the child does not properly understand his sex and prefers to emulate the opposite sex, a long series of consequences are set in motion. It is difficult for that child to socialize well or to function with confidence. Hence, he "flees" to an assumed life as the other sex or comforts himself by associating intimately only with the same sex.

87

Is there any truth to the theory that homosexual tendencies appear at an early age, as young as preschool-aged children?

Dr. Richard Fitzgibbons of the Catholic Medical Association explained the basis for an understanding of gender-identity disorder: "Children are not born knowing they are male or female or what it means to be male or female, but they are born with a drive to discover who they are and to identify with others. Once they correctly identify their own sex, they need to feel happy about who they are."[5]

Briefly, gender-identity disorder is a developmental failure to identify with one's own sex. Children with this disorder are usually pre-homosexual. A comprehensive book by Kenneth Zucker and Susan Bradley traces the steps and the *missed* steps in early childhood that lead to and enforce a failure to "connect" correctly with one's own sex.[6] Troubles other than gender-identity disorder accompany the failure to connect. Same-sex attraction disorder and "cross-dressing" are symptoms of gender-identity disorder.

Properly treated, the disorder can be overcome. With young children, it can be quickly corrected.[7] In adults, recovery is possible (see q. 129).

88

Do psychiatrists recognize gender-identity disorder?

The *Diagnostic and Statistical Manual of Mental Disorders, volume IV* (1994) includes gender-identity disorder as an identifiable disorder. Some of the following criteria are used for assessment:

- A strong and persistent cross-gender identification

- In children the manifestation of gender identity disorder presents as:

  - strong persistent preferences for cross-sex roles in make-believe play,

  - repeatedly stated desire to be, or insistence that he is, the other sex,

  - strong preferences for playmates of the other sex,

  - discomfort with the child's own sex (e.g., boys who wish they had no penis, girls who reject urination sitting down), and

  - rejection of sex-typical play (toys, games).

According to experts, "a history of gender-identity pathology (including effeminacy and chronic, extreme unmasculinity) is much more common among men who are predominately or exclusively homosexual than among men who are predominately or exclusively heterosexual."[8]

89

Isn't it true that doctors no longer consider homosexuality to be a disorder?

That depends on the doctor. There is a common assumption that medical opinion no longer views homosexual acts as deviant. That public assumption stems from the 1973 decision of the American Psychiatric Association to remove homosexuality from its list of diagnostic disorders. The board—not the membership—initiated the change of classification for homosexuality in its *Diagnostic and Statistical Manual of Mental Disorders*.

The board's decision was opposed by members who specialized in treating homosexuals. Prior to a general membership referendum on the issue, a letter went out in the name of the board, asking members not to contest the board's decision. It was learned later—after 58 percent of members voted not to oppose the decision—that the letter had been *written and paid for* by the National Gay Task Force. The vote, then, can hardly be termed a vote for medical wisdom.

90

Is the American Psychiatric Association unduly influenced by the homosexual movement?

The important point of the history of the American Psychiatric Association's declassification of homosexuality as a disorder is that a critical decision with ramifications for individuals and public policy was not made based on science or medicine. Volumes of scientific data were ignored. The association's own specialists were ignored. A successful homosexual lobbying campaign drove the movement to change the classification of homosexuality.[9] Politicizing medical decisions invalidates much of the work of the American Psychiatric Association.[10]

Elizabeth Moberly, author of *Homosexuality: A New Christian Ethic*, wrote, "This pattern of pressuring institutions and researchers to produce results favorable to homosexuals and then claiming the results as objective evidence occurs again and again in pro-gay literature and is perhaps one of the most curious features of scholarship in our times." [11]

91

Has the change in classification of homosexuality really mattered?

Yes, the change has had far-reaching and destructive consequences. Dr. Charles W. Socarides, who battled the American Psychiatric Association at the time of the re-classification, wrote that it "created injustices for the homosexual, as it belied the truth that prevented the homosexual from seeking and receiving psychoanalytic help." [12]

The declassification made it possible for homosexuals to present their lifestyle to the public as equal to heterosexuality. Movies, TV, and media began to portray homosexual pairs as "hip." Predictably, adolescents experimented with homosexual behavior or "discovered" they were bisexual.

In 1993 the *Washington Post* featured an article that detailed adolescent experimentation. "Fifty teenagers and dozens of school counselors and parents from the local area were interviewed. According to the article, teenagers said it has become 'cool' for students to proclaim they are gay or bisexual—even for some who are not. Not surprisingly, the caseload of teenagers in 'sexual identity crisis' doubled in one year. 'Everything is front page, gay and homosexual,' according to one psychologist who works with the schools. 'Kids are jumping on it. . . . [Counselors] are saying, "What are we going to do with all these kids proclaiming they are bisexual or homosexual when we know they are not?" ' " [13]

Besides the emotional and psychological damage to our youngsters that the "fashion trend" of homosexuality has wrought, it has exposed thousands to sexually transmitted diseases and AIDS. Yes, changing the classification really mattered.

92

Should we think of homosexuality as a mental disorder?

Objectively it is a disorder. Logically, homosexual acts are not ordered to the function that corresponds to their biological structure. Thus they are dis-ordered, against order, against nature. A person who engages in homosexual activity acts contrary to his biology.

Another measure is the self-destructive nature of the behavior. Homosexuals of both sexes remain fourteen times more likely to attempt suicide than heterosexuals.[14] They are three and a half times more likely to commit suicide successfully.[15] Homosexuals exhibit significantly higher rates of drug addiction and alcoholism.[16] Lesbians are three times more likely to abuse alcohol, according to *Nursing Research*.[17]

93

Is it possible that the suicide statistics of homosexuals is a reflection of their alienation from the wider culture?

Thirty years ago, this propensity toward suicide was attributed to social rejection, but the numbers have remained stable since then despite far greater public acceptance since 1973 (see q. 89). Study after study indicates that male and female homosexuals have much higher rates of interpersonal maladjustment, depression, conduct disorder, childhood abuse (both sexual and violent), domestic violence, alcohol or drug abuse, anxiety, and dependency on psychiatric care than heterosexuals.[18]

94

What other significant health concerns are there for persons with same-sex attraction?

One of the tragedies of homosexual behavior is that its victims have unnaturally short life-expectancies. The life expectancy of homosexual men was forty-eight years before the AIDS virus erupted in the homosexual community; today it is thirty-eight years.[19] Just 2 percent of homosexual men live past age sixty-five.[20] The grief of loss for their families is one more cost to a society that denies the pathology of homosexual behavior.

Other health issues are advanced rates of cancer, HIV, and sexually transmitted diseases. Male homosexuals are prone to cancer (especially anal cancer, which is quite rare among male heterosexuals) and various sexually transmitted diseases, including urethritis, laryngitis, prostatitis, hepatitis A and B, syphilis, gonorrhea, chlamydia, herpes, lymphogranuloma venereum, and genital warts (caused by human papilloma virus, which is also a cause of genital cancers).[21] Hepatitis B and C are also more prevalent in active homosexuals.[22]

Male homosexuals are particularly prone to develop sexually transmitted diseases due to near compulsive promiscuity[23] (see q. 30).

95

There are reports of a "gay-bowel syndrome." Is that a real disease or an urban myth?

Gay-bowel syndrome is a cluster of gastro-intestinal infections, including proctitis and proctocolitis (inflammation of the rectum and colon). The symptoms are described as painful bloody rectal discharges with spasms, and they are found predominately in persons engaging in anal intercourse. Enteritis (inflammation of the small intestine) may also contribute to a patient's gay-bowel syndrome discomfort. These symptoms occur in persons who engage in oral-anal acts where feces are ingested.[24]

96

Why should active homosexual men be more likely to have proctocolitis and proctitis than heterosexual men?

The rectum is not designed for sex. But when it is used in this way, the fragility of the tissue causes the rectum to tear and bleed, which is one factor that makes anal sex such an efficient means of transmitting the AIDS and hepatitis viruses.

Infection is compounded by immunological factors. Seminal fluid carries an "immuno-regulatory macromolecule," which has markers that are "read" only by the female body. This process prevents the female immune system from rejecting the incoming sperm as an invader, thus permitting fusion of the sperm and ovum resulting in conception. Researchers believe anal intercourse deposits these macromolecules in an unreceptive rectum; the sperm, confused, then fuse with other cells and can cause malignancies to develop.[25]

97

Are there different health risks for lesbians?

Many of the same health risks found in surveys of practicing homosexual men hold true for lesbians: sexually transmitted diseases, cancer, HIV, and AIDS.[26]

Lesbians are less promiscuous than gay men but more promiscuous than heterosexual women. One large study found that 42 percent of lesbians had had more than ten sexual partners.[27] A substantial percentage of them were strangers.

98

Are women who have sex exclusively with other women at less risk for sexually transmitted infections?

No. In addition to the usual list of diseases or infections, lesbians contract bacterial vaginosis. Lesbians also tend to have higher rates of attendant behaviors (such as smoking, alcohol use, drug use, and obesity) that place them at increased risk for cancer.[28]

99

What about depression? It seems that many lesbians are prone to depression.

Lesbians and homosexual men have higher rates of depression than found in the general population.[29] Lesbians share male homosexuals' propensity for drug abuse, psychiatric disorder, and suicide.[30] In one study, lesbians reported high rates of childhood abuse or incidents of physical assault.[31]

100

Isn't it logical that homosexuality is genetic? Why would someone choose to be gay?

It is extremely complicated in its particulars, but in general, research demonstrates that there is no biological basis for homosexuality.

Dean Byrd, a clinical professor of social services at Brigham Young University and the University of Utah, wrote, "Scientific attempts to demonstrate that homosexual attraction is biologically determined have failed. The major researchers now prominent in the scientific arena—themselves gay activists—have in fact arrived at such conclusions."[32]

Byrd notes the work of Dean Hamer, whose research attempted

to link male homosexuality to a stretch of DNA located at the tip of the X chromosome, the chromosome that some men inherit from their mothers. "There is not a single master gene that makes people gay. . . . I don't think we will ever be able to predict who will be gay."[33] In fact, science finds far greater evidence that a predisposition to alcoholism is genetic, yet no one advocates an "alcoholic lifestyle" as a "right" because alcoholics "are just born that way."

101

What about identical twins? Has anyone studied twins and homosexuality?

Twin studies have been made, and the results prove that homosexuality is not genetic. The research shows that environmental factors are the predominate influence on the development of same-sex attraction disorder. The premise is simple: If homosexuality is genetic, then identical twins always ought to have either heterosexual or homosexual orientations; one of the pair in a twin set cannot have a homosexual orientation while the identical twin has heterosexual orientation. Many studies report case histories in which environmental differences account for the differing patterns of sexual attraction in identical twins.[34]

102

Wasn't there a recent study that found differences in the brains of homosexual persons?

There was a widely discussed article in *Science* that made claims for a biological origin of homosexuality. The article published the study of Dr. Simon LeVay on variations in the brain structure of deceased homosexuals.[35] Activists made much of the study despite the prevailing scientific view against a biological cause for same-sex attraction. (The celebrated sex researchers Masters and

Johnson had said as far back as 1979 that homosexuals are "homosexually oriented by learned preference," adding in 1985, "The genetic theory of homosexuality has been generally discarded today." [36])

103

Was there any validity at all to the brain study that found differences in the brains of homosexual and heterosexual persons?

The LeVay study had flaws that are detailed, but briefly, methodological flaws included failure to properly set up a control group. And there were some shaky assumptions regarding which cadavers were heterosexual, despite those cadavers having AIDS. An important notation is that the nineteen "homosexual" cadavers all had the AIDS virus—hence the likelihood that this group of subjects was not a fair subset of the homosexual population. (All practicing homosexuals do not have AIDS.) [37]

LeVay himself pointed out that any correlation in sexual orientation and brain structure was not proof of *causation* of orientation. LeVay noted that it might be the other way around, that orientation and practice brought about the changes in the brain. An additional question raised by William Byne and Bruce Parsons in the *Archives of General Psychiatry* was whether the AIDS virus had caused the brain anomalies in LeVay's subjects. [38]

As with many such studies, more investigation is required before society bases its public health, public policy and laws on the findings.

104

If there is no "gay gene," then why are there so many people with same-sex attraction?

There are not "so many" people with same-sex attraction. The mythical figure of 10 percent [39] has been shattered by research. Less than half that number is homosexual.

The data, based on self-identified homosexual or bisexual subjects, demonstrates that 3 percent of males identify themselves as homosexual, and less than 2 percent of women identify themselves as lesbian.[40]

It may seem as if a higher percentage of society could be homosexual because there are many visible proponents. Academia, entertainment, and the media are currently favorable to homosexual ideology because it pushes the edge of "personal freedom" that rejects traditional morality.

105

The media frequently report that 10 percent of the population is homosexual. Where did they get that figure?

That figure is fiction. It is important to know the origins of this false percentage. The pro-homosexual publication *Journal of Homosexuality* admits that the figure is fabricated for political gain. In an article called "Size Matters," Matthew Pruitt wrote, "More gay people, quite straightforwardly, means more political clout. . . . Business and corporate decisions may be . . . influenced by the size of the gay community."[41]

106

Where did homosexual activists find the 10 percent figure?

The homosexual activists draw on what they know is not accurate —the work of Alfred Kinsey. Kinsey was a zoologist turned sexologist at Indiana University. His major work, *Sexual Behavior in the Human Male* (1948), was methodologically flawed because he surveyed suspect subject groups (male prisoners, for instance, who were likely to be imprisoned for molestation and rape). Kinsey, addicted to pornography, was a very troubled man with bizarre, psychotic sexual habits of his own.[42]

A *Newsweek* article summed up the Kinsey connection: "New

evidence suggests that ideology, not sound science, has perpetrated a one-in-ten myth. In the nearly half century since Kinsey, no survey has come close to duplicating his findings."[43] Many scientists today refer to Kinsey's work as "junk science."

But for over thirty years Kinsey's destructive work has been the basis for sex education, judges' rulings, and legislation. Citation of Kinsey's fraudulent "science" appeared in over 600 law review articles between 1982 and 2000.[44] Charles Rice, law professor at the University of Notre Dame, observed that Kinsey's research was "contrived, ideologically driven, and misleading."[45]

107

If there is no "gay gene," how does one become a homosexual person?

No one is born pre-programmed with same-sex attraction. If there are genetic indications—and that is in dispute—it is that in some people a predisposition may make them vulnerable to compromising *environmental* conditions.

This idea is similar to the case of a person born with a weak respiratory system: He may be predisposed to develop asthma if the necessary conditions are present, but if he is raised in dry heat locales, he will not develop asthma. The environment must be conducive to the development of same-sex attraction.

And that is good news, because it means that same-sex attraction is both preventable and treatable (see appendix II for a list of resources for professional help with same-sex attraction).

What's needed now is to counter the erroneous idea taught in schools that "gay" teens are to be encouraged to express their homosexuality because it is innate. Same-sex attraction is a developmental disorder that can be corrected (see q. 129). The lifestyle of the typical active homosexual is medically dangerous and emotionally devastating (see qq. 92–94). Compassion for men and women caught in this debilitating disorder demands that the truth be told and taught. The lives of these men and women should not be sacrificed to advance an ideology of moral anarchy.

108

If homosexuality is not genetic, why does anyone have same-sex attraction?

There are so many variables that a succinct answer may be a disservice. A brief sketch below indicates some of the factors involved. There are resources in appendix II that offer solid science and professional guidance.

Essentially, when a child does not identify with his father or with her mother as the model of his or her own gender, disassociation occurs: "Healthy psychological development requires that a little boy be able to feel acceptance by and identify with his father, experience acceptance by male peers, recognize that there are two sexes, and that he is male and will grow up to be a man and possibly a father, not a woman and a mother. Additionally he needs to feel good about his body and about being a boy and becoming a man. He needs to believe that his mother and father are happy that he is a boy and expect him to become a man, and he needs to feel accepted as a boy by other boys." [46]

Jeffrey Satinover, author of *Homosexuality and the Politics of Truth*, adds another piece of the outline of how the pre-homosexual child may develop inappropriate responses to his own gender: "Although he has 'defensively detached' from his father, the young boy still carries silently within him a terrible longing for the warmth, love, and encircling arms of the father he never did nor could have. Early on, he develops intense, nonsexual attachments to older boys he admires—but at a distance, repeating with them the same experience of longing and unavailability. When puberty sets in, sexual urges—which can attach themselves to any object, especially in males—rise to the surface and combine with his already intense need for masculine intimacy and warmth. He begins to develop homosexual crushes. Later he recalls, 'My first sexual longings were directed not at girls but at boys. I was never interested in girls.'

"Psychotherapeutic intervention at this point and earlier can be successful in preventing the development of later homosexuality."[47]

109

When it is claimed that same-sex attraction or gender identity disorder is a developmental problem, isn't that code-speak for blaming the parents? Wasn't the stereotype of the cold father and the smothering mother discredited years ago?

Years ago, when children of loving parents had rickets, we did not "blame" the parents, but we did learn that a proper diet and vitamin D was necessary for a baby's bones to grow properly. The unintended result of ignorance about diet was poorly developed bones.

Most parents today are very anxious to provide the best atmosphere possible for their children. The question is not about "blame" but about education. Parents should have opportunities to learn about the critical stages of gender development so that an optimum environment for development can be ensured. In the course of regular events, these developmental tasks are accomplished in the natural, tumbling busyness of family life.

Sometimes, the circumstances of life make it difficult for one or both parents to fully engage the child during that critical phase of gender-identity development. War, death, job loss, illness, absence, depression, alcoholism—many factors can affect a family at a particular moment in a child's life. The task is to insure that parent education courses and books alert parents to this critical stage of development in much the same way as parents learn when a child should take his first steps or say his first word.

110

Is it sometimes true that religious doctors attempt to fit their research to what their faith tradition teaches?

Just as there are homosexual advocates who deliberately read into their work what they want to discover, and thus skew the results or conclusions, there could be professionals whose religious thought influences their work. But it would not be necessary: For those of the Catholic tradition, there is no fear that science will invalidate the human ability to follow the moral precepts given in the Scriptures.

God is the author of all that is, including science. Science, objectively studied, will always validate God's design and plan for human beings.

5

What Does the Bible Say?

111

Are Catholics aware that some people feel oppressed by the Catholic Church? The Church issues too many statements on other people's private sex lives.

The Catholic Church must be faithful to its missionary calling: to bear witness to the world of the "good news" of salvation in Jesus Christ. Part of the good news is that people who labor under the burden of sin and its consequences *can* live in truth. The Church proclaims the truth to all.

The Church, mother of the faithful, never tires of promoting the dignity of persons. Married people are called to the fullness of their dignity when they live in fidelity to their marriage vows. When married life is marred by rejection of the truth about married life, the couple, their children, and society suffer.

A person with same-sex attraction is called to the fullness of human dignity. In no manner should any person be identified with their emotional or developmental struggles. When the society indulges an un-truth such as same-sex unions, the dignity of all is compromised.

112

What about religious freedom? You cannot require that everyone see things the same way that the Catholic Church sees them.

The Church's own decree protects the right of the person and communities to social and civil liberty in religious matters.[1] And that freedom for Christians manifests itself within public life as part of the gospel command to "go therefore and make disciples of all nations, baptizing them in the name of the Father and of the Son and of the Holy Spirit, teaching them to observe all that I have commanded you" (Matt. 28:19–20).

The Church, "the pillar and bulwark of the truth" (1 Tim. 3:15), "has received this solemn command of Christ from the apostles to announce the saving truth."[2] "To the Church belongs the right, always and everywhere, to announce moral principles, including those pertaining to the social order, and to make judgments on any human affairs to the extent that they are required by the fundamental rights of the human person or the salvation of souls."[3]

The Church cannot require any person or society to "see things as the Catholic Church sees them," but it can and must give witness to the truth and exhort all to defend that truth as individuals, families, and communities.

113

Why does the Catholic Church follow the Bible, which is an outdated Near Eastern text, as a guide to modern life? It seems pointless, doesn't it?

No, it is not pointless. It can be pointed, though. The Bible, the word of God, contains wisdom that is timeless and cannot be exhausted by any era.

114

Religious people use the Bible to justify hate speech against gays and lesbians. Whatever happened to "love your neighbor"?

It *is* an act of "love your neighbor" when Catholics and all of good will speak against the immorality of same-sex unions and the desolate homosexual "lifestyle." To offer truth to one in error is a work of fraternal correction (cf. Matt. 18:15). Proverbs warns, "He who justifies the wicked and he who condemns the righteous are both alike an abomination to the Lord" (Prov. 17:15).

115

Your own Bible says to "judge not." Why do Christians ignore the words of their God?

When Catholics are given a "judge not" warning, what they hear is "Be silent and tolerate the evil you see." The teaching of Jesus to "judge not" (Matt. 7:1–5), concludes with "First take the log out of your own eye, and then you will see clearly to take the speck out of your brother's eye." The essence of that admonition is that we must not have a judgmental attitude toward others, because "all have sinned and fall short of the glory of God" (Rom. 3:23). There is no prohibition against judging the *behavior* of others. In fact, we must admonish the sinner as one of the spiritual works of mercy.[4]

Paul provides perspective on judging. When sexual immorality was found in the community of believers, he wrote, "I have already pronounced judgment in the name of the Lord Jesus on the man who has done such a thing" (1 Cor. 5:3–4).

One absolutely may not judge the worth or eternal destiny of another—this is strictly reserved to God. But one must love the sinner enough to hate the sin that separates the sinner from God. One concrete indication of the love that the Church bears for homosexual persons is the AIDS clinics and health services that the Church builds and maintains throughout the world. Another sign of love of the Church for all caught in this particular error is the assistance offered through apostolates such as Courage.

116

Catholics seem to forget that Jesus had no trouble with all the people you judge—adulterers, prostitutes and tax collectors, remember?

He did have trouble with their *actions*. Recall that he told the woman caught in adultery to "go, and do not sin again" (John 8:11). Jesus did not applaud the woman caught in adultery for her "liberated lifestyle." Nor did he advocate making a new law to legalize prostitution so that prostitutes would not be "oppressed." Zacchaeus, whose tax-gathering defrauded his neighbors, paid it back fourfold after his encounter with Christ (cf. Luke 19:1–10)

Jesus loves. Love does not leave loved ones in sin.

117

Intolerance is a sin far worse than loving someone of the same sex, isn't it?

Should we be tolerant of purveyors of child pornography? Drunk drivers? Arsonists? What are the criteria for determining what is or is not tolerable in society? If we tolerate a practice that is intrinsically disordered, are we tolerating broken families and early death? Is this what we intend to choose as a culture?

The criteria for tolerance cannot be whatever a particular group demands. The criteria must be ordered to an objective standard. Tolerance has become a euphemism for "I'll wink at your sin if you wink at mine." Most who hide behind the guise of "tolerance" on moral issues either are mired in a deep sin of their own or fear social and economic repercussions if they take a strong moral stand.

Christians must "preach the word, be urgent in season and out of season, convince, rebuke, and exhort, be unfailing in patience and in teaching" (2 Tim. 4:2) Too many Catholics "just want to get along," and when they adopt "tolerance" as a mask for lukewarmness, the Christian is in sin.

118

But doesn't the Bible extol the virtue of tolerance?

Scripture does have something to say about tolerance: "I know . . . you cannot bear evil men" (Rev. 2:2). "For the time is coming when people will not endure sound teaching" (2 Tim. 4:3).

We can say that Scripture in its entirety is a love letter to man from God—but despite his infinite love for man, God does not tolerate sin.

Where Scripture urges tolerance, it is among brothers and sisters in Christ who are not to squabble over minor points such as dietary laws. Christians are not to allow quibbling to injure Christian unity (cf. Rom. 14:1–23). This prohibition against "judging" others who practice differently in minor matters cannot be extended to mean a tolerance of grave evils such as fornication, homosexual acts, or adultery.

119

Doesn't new scholarship indicate that the Sodom and Gomorrah account is a story about hospitality, not homosexual acts?

No reputable scholarship accepts that premise. Some have proposed that the Hebrew verb meaning "to know" can mean "become acquainted with" as well as "carnal knowledge." And it is true that the "acquainted" meaning is how the verb is used most often in Scripture.

But the "carnal knowledge" meaning is plain from the context. The events described in Genesis 19 are clear. Furthermore, it turns God into a monster who would destroy two cities for a failure to be hospitable. In verse 7, Lot pleads with the men who surround his house demanding to have sex with his male visitors: "I beg you, my brothers, do not act so wickedly." So wicked were those homosexual acts that Lot offered the mob his own virginal daughters instead. That is hardly something a man would offer to a mob that only wanted to be "acquainted" with his visitors. It is not possible to find a breach of hospitality in Sodom as the cause of God's wrath. God destroyed the cities because the sin of sodomy was so "very grave" (Gen. 18:20), and not even ten righteous men could be found in the city (cf. Gen. 18:32).

Mention should be made of Jude 7, which says that Sodom and Gomorrah were destroyed for "unnatural lust," not a failure of hospitality.

120

Homosexual rape was Sodom's sin, not loving same-sex relationships.[5] No one denounces heterosexual relations just because there are incidents of rape. Why penalize homosexual partners?

Since the publication in 1955 of D. Sherwin Bailey's book *Homosexuality and the Western Christian Tradition*, some researchers have attempted to make the plain sense of the Genesis verses read as "sins of hospitality" or as homosexual rape, which is about an act of domination, not a loving act of same-sex union.

The best approach to the clear meaning of the Old Testament account of the destruction of Sodom and Gomorrah is not found in speculation driven by ideology. The better approach is to read the New Testament to understand how the gospel writers and the apostles understood the Sodom text. In 2 Peter, the context of the apostle's warning is of false prophets and a life of "licentiousness, and because of them the way of truth will be reviled" (2 Pet. 2:2). Peter takes aim at Sodom: God destroyed Sodom as a warning to others who would follow their wicked "licentious" ways. There is no distinction whatever in the text between homosexual "domination" (rape) or homosexual "partners." The sin of Sodom was not aggression; it was licentiousness.[6]

Most helpful is to know the full range of references to homosexuality in Scripture, especially Leviticus. Men were forbidden to "lie with a male as with a woman; it is an abomination" (Lev. 18:22). And further, "if a man lies with a male as with a woman, both of them have committed an abomination; they shall be put to death, their blood is upon them" (Lev. 20:13). Again, there is no distinction between aggressive homosexual rape versus "loving" relationships. In fact, the text indicates that both are to be put to death. The text makes no exception for any emotional motivation of the act. Clearly, God did not have in mind a dispensation for "loving" homosexual partners.

121

The prophet Ezekiel said Sodom was destroyed because it was rich and haughty—no homosexuality in that condemnation. Why leave out that point?

Ezekiel 16:49–50 also lists alongside Sodom's wealth and deafness toward the poor the fact that the people of Sodom "did abominable things before me." *Abomination* is a term most often reserved in Scripture for idolatry, child sacrifice, and sexual sins. Numerous other verses make clear that Sodom's sins included homosexuality (see appendix I).

122

Don't the lists of "abominations" mainly refer to ritual uncleanness —for religious purposes—not for private life?

That supposition, theorized by homosexual activists, is not supported in the context of the verses in Leviticus 18–20. Chapter 18 outlines various forbidden sexual practices, including verse 22 forbidding men to lie with men and verse 25 warning that such acts even make the land unclean. The abomination of homosexuality is located between child sacrifice (v. 21) and bestiality (v. 23). These are hardly acts that are merely ritually unclean.

Homosexual acts are unnatural; that is, they violate the natural design and function of human sexuality. One need not be "religious" to understand this principle.

123

Do we know that Sodom was destroyed expressly for homosexual sins, or did God destroy "rich and haughty" Sodom for its many sins?

Yes, Sodom was destroyed for its many sins, but chief among them was rampant homosexuality. The first-century historian Josephus confirms this understanding of God's message in the destruction of Sodom and Gomorrah.[7] Consider the similar case in Judges 19–21.

124

Homosexual acts are condemned in certain Old Testament books, but haven't we learned that it was because of the connection with worship of other gods, not because there is anything intrinsically wrong with homosexual acts?

No, that deflection by homosexual apologists cannot bear the weight of their argument. The cult practice of homosexual prostitution associated with the worship of false gods is not the only factor for the absolute prohibition against homosexual acts. In Leviticus homosexual acts are also located in the list of forbidden practices we still prohibit: adultery, incest, and bestiality.

125

Isn't it true that the prohibitions in the Old Testament no longer hold for New Testament theology? We don't keep the dietary laws, for instance.

The Old Testament prohibitions against homosexual acts are repeated in New Testament theology by Paul (cf. Rom. 1:26–28, 32; 1 Cor. 6:9–10) and Peter (2 Peter 2). Both repeat the condemnation of homosexual acts, adultery, fornication, incest, and bestiality.

Do not confuse Old Testament ceremonial laws with *moral* absolutes. Moral laws are based on God's design for the earth and the human person, made in the image of God. They are valid for all time. God gave man and woman to each other in a bond so exclusive that it supersedes even the bond with one's own parents. The anatomical design, ordered to a true and fruitful union, is not to be defiled with unnatural acts. "Populating the earth with humans is a precondition for ruling it, and procreation is a precondition for filling the earth. The complementarity of the male and female is thereby secured in the divinely sanctioned work of governing creation. . . . The fullness of God's 'image' comes together in the union of the male and female in marriage."[8]

126

Wasn't the relationship of David and Jonathan a homosexual love affair?

No. The relationship between David and King Saul's son Jonathan was sealed in three covenants as brothers and political allies (cf. 1 Sam. 23:16–18). Some have tried to twist the "love-language" between David and Jonathan into a homoerotic love song, but on close examination it is clear that these men had a "soul bond" (cf. 1 Sam. 18:1–5) as close brothers. The same "soul bond" is found in Genesis 44:30–31 between a father (Jacob) and his son (Benjamin). Fraternal friendship between David and Jonathan is deep and lasting but not sexual.

127

David mourns for Jonathan and explicitly says that his love was "wonderful, passing the love of women" (2 Sam. 1:26). Why do Catholics try to ignore this clear evidence of their homosexual relationship?

David and Jonathan were not lovers. The passage in 2 Samuel is endearing and indicative of deep grief, for Jonathan had given his life and his inheritance to David in utter loyalty—utter love—a love "more wonderful" than a woman, in that no woman (wife) could have been more loyal or selfless. Overblown attempts to make a case for a homosexual relationship are deflated easily. The claim that the Old Testament narrator tried to suppress the truth of the relationship and delicately "implied" it—instead of condemning it outright as in Genesis, Leviticus, Deuteronomy, and Judges—is not sustained. The narrator is at great pains to *show* the depth of their brotherly love, not "suppress" it.[9]

6

Political Considerations

128

Is there any hope for a Christian person who struggles with same-sex attraction?

There is solid hope for persons who want to live chastely or even consider reparative therapy.[1] The difficulty is that the message about hope is obstructed by the politicized debate. The homosexual lobby wants to prevent any discussion of being "ex-gay" for the simple reason that if it is shown that people can and do leave the gay lifestyle, then it compromises their foundation that people are "born gay" and that they are doing what is "natural" for them.

Many people have moved beyond their homosexual orientation to become happy, well-adjusted heterosexuals. The medical community is awakening to the understanding that homosexual persons have a right to be advised that psychological counseling is available for those who want to retrace some of their developmental detours.

129

What is reparative therapy, and does it really work?

Reparative therapy (also called re-orientation therapy) makes a distinction between the homosexual person and being "gay"; the latter is a cultural-political identity based on sexual orientation. Therapy begins with the assumption that homosexual persons are not "born gay," but neither did they "choose" their orientation. A complex confluence of circumstances during the critical developmental years from birth to about six years is responsible for gender-identity disorder and same-sex attraction disorder. Children with gender confusion or same-sex attraction are vulnerable to "gays" who promote a homosexual lifestyle. But many homosexual persons experience the "gay lifestyle" as destructive, unacceptable medically and socially, or a violation of their religious beliefs. Some have sought therapy to address those developmental issues that originated in childhood.[2]

Reparative therapy has a good success rate among those who voluntarily seek this model of therapy, though change is not quick nor without some conflict and anxiety.

One prominent study of reparative therapy was conducted by Dr. Robert Spitzer, a former "pro-gay" psychiatrist and researcher. Spitzer's data was collected from men and women who actively chose to seek help for their disorder. Sixty-seven percent of the men and 35 percent of the women cited hopes for marriage and family or the desire to remain married as a primary motivation for therapy.[3]

Complete re-orientation is difficult. After therapy, some people report occasional attractions for persons of the same sex. But an attraction for a person of the same sex does not have to result in sexual activity. In the same manner that one may experience a desire to indulge other emotions, one more often chooses self-control and thus re-directs one's interests. Most patients report satisfaction with the results of reparative therapy.

Some have suggested that reparative therapy is a dangerous attempt to change a natural inclination. Spitzer found the opposite. Patients reported that therapy had benefits for growth and maturity in several areas of their lives in addition to their sexual orientation. Homosexual persons, their families, clergy, and professionals should understand that the attempt to censor proponents of reparative therapy is politically motivated and is not supported by the scientific data. Furthermore, continued research into the developmental causes of homosexuality is an urgent need because "wiser parenting would aid in prevention of homosexual development."[4]

130

What about teens who suddenly announce that they are gay?

Teens have suffered an unconscionable assault by the education establishment. The homosexual lobby has successfully pressed schools and colleges to teach that homosexuality is as appropriate as heterosexuality. Once again, a politicized effort to change the culture is launched at the expense of millions of innocent teens.

Same-sex attractions do not "prove" that one is a homosexual. Some adolescents have temporary encounters with same-gender friends. Tragically, the immediate assumption is "I'm gay" and, unless aided by a wise adult, the young person may soon find himself struggling against unwanted sexual disorder. Parents, teachers, and pastors can do much to assist young people who question their orientation.

The Catholic Medical Association has a booklet called *Homosexuality and Hope* that is of interest to anyone who needs and wants straight answers for tough questions. The National Association of Research and Therapy of Homosexuality also has a wealth of information, hundreds of studies, an advocacy outreach, and reliable referrals to medical professionals dedicated to the mental health of homosexual persons. These associations are courageous witnesses to truth in a political environment in which social tension and pressure to accept the homosexual "lifestyle" increases daily.

131

Is there an organized homosexual agenda?

There is a well-coordinated and financed homosexual agenda. A blueprint of the inner working of the homosexual movement is revealed in *After the Ball*, a book written by two homosexual activists. *After the Ball* outlines eight principles to overturn "straight America." Principle five is "Portray Gays as Victims, not as Aggressive Challengers."[5] "Gays" are not victims; they are not denied education, employment, or access to courts, nor are they denied any civil rights. The plan specifically advises activists to present themselves as victims of prejudice.

Principle eight is to craft images that "make the victimizers look bad." Examples given are: "hysterical backwoods preachers, drooling with hate to a degree that looks both comical and deranged" and "menacing punks . . . who speak coolly about the 'fags' they have bashed or would like to bash."[6]

There are numerous so-called "gay positive" organizations and associations dedicated to the social, cultural, and political acceptance of a fully homosexualized culture. The assault on the culture includes dividing churches on the matter of same-sex unions and other political goals of the homosexual agenda.

132

Is the homosexual agenda being promoted internationally?

Yes. Homosexual organizations are operative in many nations, particularly Europe. In fact, Europe has exported its permissive agenda to other countries, including the United States.

An example of European influence on the United States is best illustrated by the Supreme Court's decision in the *Lawrence v. Texas* case that overturned a Texas sodomy law. An amicus brief was filed by Mary Robinson of Ireland, former United Nations high commissioner of human rights. Robinson led the campaign for homosexual law reform in Ireland. Her efforts were rewarded. The majority opinion on Lawrence cited the values of the "wider community," including the European Court of Human Rights and its "affirmation of the protected right of homosexual adults to engage in intimate consensual conduct."[7]

Justice Antonin Scalia wrote in dissent, "Today's opinion is the product of a Court, which is the product of a law-profession culture, that has largely signed on to the so-called homosexual agenda, by which I mean the agenda promoted by some homosexual activists directed at eliminating the moral opprobrium that has traditionally attached to homosexual conduct."[8]

A second example of the international pressure exerted by the homosexual agenda involved the flagship international institution, the United Nations. During the summer of 2004, activists convinced the United Nations to approve employee benefits for same-sex pairs whose arrangement was legal in their home country. The policy was implemented over the objections of most member states, particularly Catholic and Islamic nations.

Pro-family activists at the U.N. have fought to keep the phrase "various forms of family" out of official (binding) U.N. documents. But groups such as the International Gay and Lesbian Human Rights Commission, led by Paula Ettelbrick (see q. 18), are persistent. Family advocates know that the phrase is a mask for homosexual "marriages." If such "forms of family" are legalized, Catholics and others of traditional faiths will find that their values are suddenly on the wrong side of international law. Already a Canadian court has upheld a 2001 ruling against a man who submitted a newspaper ad that quoted Bible verses that prohibit homosexuality.[9]

133

What will legalized same-sex unions mean to Catholics?

Catholic religious freedom is in very grave danger. If such unions become the law of the land, all Catholic employers, teachers, doctors, landlords, and many other professions will be expected to apply or implement provisions of the law that are in direct conflict with Catholic moral principles.

Parents will face agonizing choices over how or if to expose their children to public schools. Catholic schools will be asked to use texts that are designed to corrupt the most innocent young minds. Pastors may be prohibited from preaching against homosexuality from the pulpit or in catechetical classes. In Sweden and Canada pastors have already been censored and fined for doing just that.

Conclusion

The cultural battle for the preservation of marriage is not one of religion, politics, geography, or ethnicity. Marriage is, quite simply, the human future.

Proponents of same-sex unions have persuaded much of the public that such unions are a matter of "justice," a matter of "rights." The same voices for "diversity" shout down scholars and medical experts who offer hope for those who struggle with homosexuality. Experts have demonstrated that homosexual tendencies and same-sex attraction disorder can be prevented. Effective parental education and early childhood counseling can save thousands from a lifetime of sexual confusion and personal grief. Yet this truth is unwelcome in public discourse, ridiculed in academia, and discarded by public policy makers. Why is this information suppressed?

Once a culture has vested too much of itself in an error, that error is costly to disassemble. Sexual license has spawned multibillion dollar industries. Educational grants and think-tank foundations drive much of the public discourse and most of governmental policy on matters of sexuality. Corporations with much to lose if America recovers her virtue pour millions into "research" that supports the sexually permissive culture. If college professors teach it, corporations fund it, and the government legalizes it, can it be wrong?

Hedonism is an addictive elixir. Heterosexuals engaged in "serial monogamy" as a lifestyle of revolving relationships are quick to endorse the "rights" of homosexual activists. If the whole of society is "free" to design any lifestyle of one's preference, then *none* can be held to any standard. Many assume that the "old virtue" was necessary because the consequences of sexual permissiveness endangered others. Today, with science as mid-wife, a new paradigm of virtue is born.

Modern cultures are tempted to believe that science can erase the consequences of immoral lifestyles, either heterosexual or homosexual. But virtue is part of the recognition of immutable truths. True virtue is a life lived as a reflection of the world that we have been given and did not create ourselves. This "given-ness" is the truth that we cannot change—and thus we choose to obey.

Virtue must be both personal and public in order to give structure to the society. Minus this vital structure, chaos reigns.

The most trenchant enemy of marriage is a virulent hedonism given free reign in a permissive culture. The demand for same-sex union is the logical result of a culture addicted to sexual license, a culture that attacks the virtue and morality on which a free society depends. That attack on virtue is, in the final analysis, the hubris of a scientific materialism in rebellion against the created order.

Marriage and family, love and sex, reflect God's love of mankind as well as his design embedded in all of creation. Sex is intrinsically symbolic in that it joins two opposite, but complementary, entities to form a unified whole. The imagery of wholeness —completeness—is an ordered view of reality in which Christ draws all things to himself. For Catholics the concept of wholeness as the fruit of the union between distinct entities touches on deeper theology: the union of body and soul, nature and grace, human and divine.

To thwart the design and function of human sexuality necessarily hurtles mankind down a blind alleyway of history that may take centuries to retrace. Collectively all cultures know this reality (it is written into the being of every person), yet modernity has rebelled against this "known but forgotten" truth. If society rejects the intrinsic meaning and purpose of human sexuality and the conjugal embrace of male and female, it is also forced to reject life as having any meaning beyond whatever pleasure can be wrested from it.

In the name of "tolerance" or "rights," we are persuaded to ignore the precipice of nihilistic practices such as contraception, abortion, and homosexuality. Various substitutions for true marital unity brought modern culture too many misshapen relationships marred by alienation and compounded by promiscuous, nameless encounters. Only in married intimacy can the joining of two persons, male and female, express a relationship that— transcending ephemeral pleasure—is an image of an eternal truth.

On a practical level, it should be noted that same-sex unions are not sustainable. A glance at Europe proves that where such practices have been accepted birthrates plummet below replacement. Europe is further along the road paved by the domino effect: first contraception, then abortion, followed by divorce, cohabitation, and promiscuity, and finally open homosexual practice. Family is no longer the summit of societal life. Loss of human capital requires the importation of "guest workers" who soon bring tension and cultural change to the host culture. Over time, the host culture dies out, and the immigrants replace the suicidal "sexual revolution" society.

The same holds true for religious societies. Every Protestant denomination that has cooperated with the sexual revolution is dying. Those religions that celebrate and protect marriage and family survive. It is that simple.

At the legal level, the issue of same-sex unions very quickly threatens the rights and liberties of the majority of citizens. The threat is particularly acute for people whose religious faith adheres to the prohibitions against homosexual acts given in Scripture. Will Catholic colleges be required to provide "married student housing" for same-sex couples? Will Catholic elementary schools be forced to teach from *Heather Has Two Mommies*, a second-grade textbook explaining lesbian motherhood? Will Catholic landlords be forced to rent units to same-sex couples even where the building is otherwise leased by families? Will priests be jailed for "hate crimes" because they preached against homosexual acts?

Same-sex marriage has no lasting future. But until society defeats this misguided understanding of human sexuality, it will spawn societal discord. The potential for persecution of traditional families cannot be discounted. The task ahead is to educate family, friends, associates, and co-workers about the truth of marriage and society. Many do not grasp the magnitude of the threat to the culture. They do not understand that approval of same-sex unions is the death of marriage.

The enemies of marriage work tirelessly to dismantle the "unjust structure" of traditional marriage. We, the defenders, can be no less determined to fight in academia, business, the arts, media, the voting booth, and the neighborhood for the defense of the most precious institution of all human societies: marriage and family.

Appendix I:

Scriptural References for Homosexuality

Quotations are from the Revised Standard Version: Catholic Edition.

Genesis 1:27–28 and Genesis 2:18–24 set forth God's clear model of marriage as the covenant bond of a man and a woman for the purpose of deep friendship ("It is not good that the man should be alone") and procreation ("Be fruitful and multiply"). Jesus makes clear in Mark 10:6–9 that the understanding of marriage and sexual union ("the two will become one flesh") is "from the beginning," that is, since the creation of man and woman. That model is the subject of hundreds of Scripture verses in both the Old and New Testaments.

This list is confined to specific references to same-sex intercourse. (The word *homosexuality* is a recent term; it is not found in the Bible.) Citations refer to the full passage for context; text contains only the relevant verses.

Genesis 19:4–8

But before they lay down, the men of the city, the men of Sodom, both young and old, all the people to the last man, surrounded the house; and they called to Lot, "Where are the men who came to you tonight? Bring them out to us, that we may know them." Lot went out of the door to the men, shut the door after him, and said, "I beg you, my brothers, do not act so wickedly. Behold, I have two daughters who have not known man; let me bring them out to you, and do to them as you please; only do nothing to these men, for they have come under the shelter of my roof."

Leviticus 18:22-25

You shall not lie with a male as with a woman; it is an abomination. And you shall not lie with any beast and defile yourself with it, neither shall any woman give herself to a beast to lie with it: it is perversion. Do not defile yourselves by any of these things, for by all these the nations I am casting out before you defiled themselves; and the land became defiled, so that I punished its iniquity, and the land vomited out its inhabitants.

Leviticus 20:13

If a man lies with a male as with a woman, both of them have committed an abomination; they shall be put to death, their blood is upon them.

Judges 19:22-24

As they were making their hearts merry, behold, the men of the city, base fellows, beset the house round about, beating on the door; and they said to the old man, the master of the house, "Bring out the man who came into your house, that we may know him." And the man, the master of the house, went out to them and said to them, "No, my brethren, do not act so wickedly; seeing that this man has come into my house, do not do this vile thing. Behold, here are my virgin daughter and his concubine; let me bring them out now. Ravish them and do with them what seems good to you; but against this man do not do so vile a thing."

Ezekiel 16:56-58

Was not your sister Sodom a byword in your mouth in the day of your pride, before your wickedness was uncovered? Now you have become like her an object of reproach for the daughters of Edom and all her neighbors, and for the daughters of the Philistines, those round about who despise you. You bear the penalty of your lewdness and your abominations, says the Lord.

Romans 1:24–27

Therefore God gave them up in the lusts of their hearts to impurity, to the dishonoring of their bodies among themselves, because they exchanged the truth about God for a lie and worshiped and served the creature rather than the Creator, who is blessed for ever! Amen. For this reason God gave them up to dishonorable passions. Their women exchanged natural relations for unnatural, and the men likewise gave up natural relations with women and were consumed with passion for one another, men committing shameless acts with men and receiving in their own persons the due penalty for their error.

1 Corinthians 6:9–10

Do you not know that the unrighteous will not inherit the kingdom of God? Do not be deceived; neither the immoral, nor idolaters, nor adulterers, nor sexual perverts, nor thieves, nor the greedy, nor drunkards, nor revilers, nor robbers will inherit the kingdom of God.

1 Corinthians 7:2

But because of the temptation to immorality, each man should have his own wife and each woman her own husband. [This verse indicates that there is no Christian model for sexual activity outside of marriage between a man and a woman.]

1 Timothy 1:10

Immoral persons, sodomites, kidnapers, liars, perjurers, and whatever else is contrary to sound doctrine. . . .

2 Peter 2:2, 6–7, 9–10

And many will follow their licentiousness, and because of them the way of truth will be reviled. . . . If by turning the cities of Sodom and Gomorrah to ashes he condemned them to extinction and made them an example to those who were to be ungodly; and if he rescued righteous Lot, greatly distressed by the licentiousness of the wicked. . . . then the Lord knows how to . . . keep the unrighteous under punishment until the day of judgment, and especially those who indulge in the lust of defiling passion and despise authority. Bold and willful, they are not afraid to revile the glorious ones.

Jude 7–8

Just as Sodom and Gomorrah and the surrounding cities, which likewise acted immorally and indulged in unnatural lust, serve as an example by undergoing a punishment of eternal fire. Yet in like manner these men in their dreamings defile the flesh, reject authority, and revile the glorious ones.

Appendix II:

Resources

Organizations

Couple to Couple League

Natural family planning assistance, marriage building. Local chapters, seminars, and resources.

P.O. Box 111184
Cincinnati, OH 45211-1184
(513) 471-2000
www.ccli.org

One More Soul

Apostolate for couples, clergy, and physicians interested in fostering an openness to life. Referrals to physicians with natural family planning–only practice and information on sterilization reversal.

1846 N. Main Street
Dayton, OH 45405-3832
(800) 307-7685
www.omsoul.com

Pope Paul VI Institute

Dedicated to the study of human reproduction. Educational resources on ethical means to assist fertility and address reproductive disorders. Patient services include infertility assessment and reversal of tubal ligation.

6901 Mercy Road
Omaha, NE 68106-2604

(402) 390-6600
www.popepaulvi.com

Edith Stein Foundation

Promotes genuine reproductive health for women. Valuable research on the harmful physical and psychological effects of contraception.

3366 NW Expressway, Bldg. D #630
Oklahoma City, OK 73112
(405) 917-5500
www.the-edith-stein-foundation.com

John Paul II Institute for Studies on Marriage and Family

Dedicated to understand more fully the person, marriage, and family in the light of divine revelation.

Catholic University of America
415 Michigan Avenue, NE
Washington, DC 20017
(202) 526-3799
www.johnpaulii.edu

Catholic Marriage Preparation

Nonprofit Catholic marriage preparation apostolate. Mission: "To help engaged couples build their marriage on the rock of Christ in a pagan society, through the teachings of the Catholic Church. To give the necessary tools for a fulfilling life-long commitment. To teach the couples to welcome God as part of their marriage."

1109 N. Institute Street
Colorado Springs, CO 80903
(866) 425-7193
www.catholicmarriagepreponline.com

Courage

Apostolate of the Roman Catholic Church, "ministers to those with same-sex attractions and their loved ones." Endorsed by the Pontifical Council for the Family.

Church of St. John the Baptist
210 W. 31st Street
New York, NY 10001
http://couragerc.net/
(212) 268-1010

Encourage

A ministry within Courage dedicated to the spiritual needs of parents, siblings, children, and other relatives and friends of persons who have same-sex attractions.

National Association for Research and Therapy of Homosexuality

"Goal is to make effective psychological therapy available to all homosexual men and women who seek change."

16633 Ventura Boulevard, Suite 1340
Encino, CA 91436-1801
(818) 789-4440
www.narth.com

Catholic Medical Association

Mission: To uphold the principles of Catholic faith and morality as related to the science and practice of medicine. Resource for physicians, parents, clergy, and individuals who seek to address medical and psychological issues of homosexuality from the Catholic perspective. Local and regional chapters.

159 Washington Street, Suite 3
Boston, MA 02135

(617) 782-3356
www.cathmed.org

Jews Offering New Alternatives to Homosexuality

Online library, support groups.
P.O. Box 313
Jersey City, NJ 07303
(201) 433-3444
www.jonahweb.org

People Can Change

Online support group for those with same-sex attraction who seek
re-orientation.

(434) 985-8551
www.peoplecanchange.com

Appendix III:

Suggested Reading

Books

Abad, Javier, and E. Fenoy. *Marriage: A Path to Sanctity.* New York: Scepter Publishers, 1997.

Asci, Donald P. *The Conjugal Act As a Personal Act: A Study of the Catholic Concept of the Conjugal Act in the Light of Christian Anthropology.* San Francisco: Ignatius Press, 2002.

Burke, Cormac. *Covenanted Happiness: Love and Commitment in Marriage.* San Francisco: Ignatius Press, 1999.

Dailey, Timothy J. *Dark Obsession: The Tragedy and Threat of the Homosexual Lifestyle.* Nashville, Tenn.: Broadman and Holman, 2003.

Garcia de Haro, Ramon et al. *Marriage and the Family in the Documents of the Magisterium: A Course in the Theology of Marriage.* San Francisco: Ignatius Press, 1993.

Harvey, John F. *The Homosexual Person: New Thinking in Pastoral Care.* San Francisco: Ignatius Press, 1987.

———. *The Truth About Homosexuality: The Cry of the Faithful.* San Francisco: Ignatius Press, 1996.

Harvey, John F., and Gerard V. Bradley. *Same-Sex Attraction: A Parents' Guide.* South Bend, Ind.: St. Augustine's Press, 2003.

Hogan, Richard M., and John M. LeVoir. *Covenant of Love: Pope John Paul II on Sexuality, Marriage, and Family in the Modern World.* San Francisco: Ignatius Press, 1992.

Medina-Estevez, Jorge. *Male and Female He Created Them: On Marriage and the Family*. San Francisco: Ignatius Press, 2004.

Nicolosi, Joseph. *Healing Homosexuality: Case Stories of Reparative Therapy*. Northvale, N.J.: Jason Aronson, Inc., 1997.

———. *Reparative Therapy of Male Homosexuality: A New Clinical Approach*. Northvale, N.J.: Jason Aronson, Inc., 1991.

Noll, Stephen F. *Two Sexes, One Flesh: Why the Church Cannot Bless Same-Sex Marriage*. Dallas: Latimer Press, 1997.

Satinover, Jeffrey. *Homosexuality and the Politics of Truth*. North Dartmouth, Mass.: Baker Books, 1996.

Smith, Janet E. *Why Humanae Vitae Was Right: A Reader*. San Francisco: Ignatius Press, 1993.

van den Aardweg, G. J. M. *The Battle for Normality: A Guide for (Self-)Therapy for Homosexuality*. San Francisco: Ignatius Press, 1997.

Waite, Linda J. et al. *Does Divorce Make People Happy? Findings from a Study of Unhappy Marriages*. New York: Institute for American Values, 2002.

West, Christopher. *Good News About Sex and Marriage: Answers to Your Honest Questions about Catholic Teaching*. Charis Books, 2000.

———. *Theology of the Body Explained: A Commentary on John Paul II's "Gospel of the Body."* Boston: Pauline Books and Media, 2003.

Wojtyla, Karol (John Paul II), and H. T. Willets. *Love and Responsibility*. San Francisco: Ignatius Press, 1993.

Wolfe, Christopher. *Same-Sex Matters: The Challenge of Homosexuality*. Dallas: Spence Publishing, 2000.

———, ed. *Homosexuality and American Public Life*. Dallas: Spence Publishing, 1999.

Articles

Bennett, William J. "Gay Marriage: Not a Very Good Idea" (http://catholiceducation.org/articles/homosexuality/ho0013.html).

Bradley, Gerard V. "Same-Sex Unions: The End of Marriage?" (www.catholic.net/rcc/Periodicals/Dossier/2001-04/column3.html).

Budziszewski, J. "But What Do I Say?" (http://catholiceducation.org/articles/homosexuality/ho0035.html).

Dailey, Timothy J. "Homosexuality and Children: The Impact for Future Generations" (www.frc.org/get.cfm?i=WA03I33).

Fagan, Patrick. "A 'Culture' of Inverted Sexuality" (http://catholiceducation.org/articles/sexuality/se0049.html).

Gagnon, Robert A. J. "The Bible and Homosexual Practice: Theology, Analogies and Genes" (www.theologymatters.com/TMIssues/NovDec01.PDF).

George, Robert P. "One Man, One Woman" (http://catholiceducation.org/articles/marriage/mf0045.html).

McInerny, Ralph. "Apostolate to the Homosexual" (www.catholic.net/rcc/Periodicals/Dossier/2001-04/editorial.html).

Nicolosi, Linda Ames. "Historic Gay Advocate Now Believes Change is Possible" (www.narth.com/docs/spitzer3.html).

———. "Rationale for Sexual Reorientation Therapy" (www.narth.com/docs/jmft.html).

Ramsey Colloquium, "The Homosexual Movement: A Response by the Ramsey Colloquium" (www.firstthings.com/ftissues/ft9403/articles/homo.html).

Satinover, Jeffrey. "Testimony Before the Massachusetts Senate Committee Studying Gay Marriage" (http://catholiceducation.org/articles/homosexuality/h0092.html).

Shea, John et al. " 'Gay Marriage' and Homosexuality: Some Medical Comments" (lifesite.net/features/marriage_defence/SSM_MD_evidence.htm).

Smith, Janet E. "Marriage Preparation" (www.aodonline.org/aodonline-sqlimages/SHMS/Faculty/SmithJanet/Publications/ColumnsInDossier/MarraigePreperation.pdf).

Spalding, Matthew. "A Defining Moment: Marriage, the Courts, and the Constitution" (www.heritage.org/Research/LegalIssues/bg1759.cfm).

Spero, Aryeh. "Opposition to Gay Marriage is Not Discrimination" (www.aim.org/publications/guest_columns/spero/2004/mar03.html).

Throckmorton, Warren, Gary Welton, and Mike Ingram. "A Critical Review of the GLSEN Same-Sex Marriage Curriculum" (http://catholiceducation.org/articles/education/samesexcur.pdf).

Williams, L. A. "Former Lesbian and Teacher Fights Homosexual Agenda in Schools" (http://catholiceducation.org/articles/homosexuality/h0049.html).

Young, Katherine, and Paul Nathanson. "Answering Advocates of Gay Marriage" (http://catholiceducation.org/articles/homosexuality/h0064.html).

Tapes

Bernhoft, Robin. *Why a Man and a Woman?*, Johnstown, Pa.: National Parents Commission, 2003.

Church Documents

Congregation for the Doctrine of the Faith. *Letter to the Bishops of the Catholic Church on the Pastoral Care of Homosexual Persons.* October 1, 1986.

———. *Considerations Regarding Proposals to Give Legal Recognition to Unions between Homosexual Persons.* June 3, 2003.

Notes

Chapter 1: Same-Sex Unions and Society

[1] Harold J. Morowitz, "Hiding in the Hammond Report," *Hospital Practice* 10 (1975): 35–9; Catherine E. Ross, John Mirowsky and Karen Goldsteen, "The Impact of the Family on Health: Decade in Review," *Journal of Marriage and the Family* 52 (1990): 1061; Bernard L. Cohen and I-Sing Lee, "A Catalog of Risks," *Health Physics* 36 (1979): 707–22; Howard S. Gordon and Gary E. Rosenthal, "Impact of Marital Status on Hospital Outcomes: Evidence from an Academic Medical Center," *Archives of Internal Medicine* 155 (1995): 2465–71; Sheldon Cohen et al., "Social Ties and Susceptibility to the Common Cold," *Journal of the American Medical Association* 277 (1997): 1940–4.

[2] Nadine F. Marks and James D. Lambert, "Marital Status Continuity and Change among Young and Midlife Adults: Longitudinal Effects on Psychological Well-Being," *Journal of Family Issues* 19 (1998): 652–86; Alan V. Horowitz, Helene Raskin White, and Sandra Holwell-White, "Becoming Married and Mental Health: A Longitudinal Study of a Cohort of Young Adults," *Journal of Marriage and the Family* 58 (1996): 895–907.

[3] James Hitchcock, "Marriage: Why We Care" (www.wf-f.org/ JFH-Marriage.html).

[4] Pew Research Center for the People and the Press, "Gay Marriage a Voting Issue, but Mostly for Opponents" (http://people-press.org/reports/ print.php3?PageID=790).

[5] "Morality Continues to Decay," *Barna Research* (www.barna.org/ FlexPage.aspx?Page=BarnaUpdate&BarnaUpdateID=152).

[6] See "Hate Crime Statistics, 2002" at www.fbi.gov/ucr/hatecrime2002.pdf.

[7] Lettie L. Lockhart, "Letting out the Secret: Violence in Lesbian Relationships," *Journal of Interpersonal Violence* 9 (1994): 469–92.

[8] Gregory L. Greenwood et al., "Battering Victimization among Probability-based Sample of Men Who Have Sex with Men," *American Journal of Public Health* 92 (December 2002): 1966–7, quoted in Timothy J. Dailey, Peter Sprigg, *Getting It Straight: What the Research Shows About Homosexuality* (Washington, D.C.: Family Research Council, 2004), 106–7.

[9] Bureau of Justice Statistics, *Intimate Partner Violence*, National Crime Victimization Survey, U.S. Department of Justice, Washington, D.C., May 2000, pp. 4–5, 11.

[10] Robert Bork, *Slouching Towards Gomorrah* (New York: ReganBooks, 1997), 11.

[11] *Catechism of the Catholic Church* 1888.

[12] Pius XII, Address at Pentecost, June 1, 1941.

[13] Toward Tradition is "a national movement of Jewish and Christian co-operation, fighting anti-religious bigotry and secular fundamentalism."

[14] CCC 2358.

[15] Ibid., 2347.

[16] Regulations are applied equally to all groups and include prohibitions against bigamy and incest.

[17] Where cultures permit more than one sexual partner for the male, the system is more properly called concubinage. There is usually one wife who enjoys seniority and whose sons are first in the line of inheritance.

[18] Peter Lubin and Dwight Duncan, "Follow the Footnote or the Advocate as Historian of Same-Sex Marriage," *Catholic University Law Review* 47 (Summer 1998): 1300. Lubin and Duncan respond to William Eskridge, professor of jurisprudence at Yale Law School, whose conjecture that homosexual marriages were a feature of some ancient cultures is popular among supporters of homosexual unions.

[19] Cornelius Tacitus, *The Annals* XV, 37 (www.ourcivilisation.com/smartboard/shop/tacitusc/annals/chap15.htm).

[20] Helena Smith, "Love and Sex in Ancient Greece" (http://news.bbc.co.uk/1/hi/world/europe/428798.stm).

[21] John Boswell, *Same-Sex Unions in Premodern Europe* (New York: Villard Books, 1994).

[22] "The material on which Boswell built his case is the little-known 'sacrament of brotherhood' of the Eastern Orthodox Church, which provides a blessing of friendship for persons of the same sex or opposite sexes" (Elizabeth Moberly, "Homosexuality and the Truth," *First Things*, March 1997, 33).

[23] Robin Darling Young, "Gay Marriage: Reimagining Church History," *First Things*, November 1994, 43–8.

[24] Ibid.

[25] Ibid.

[26] Catholics must ask themselves if "live and let live" is code-speak for the moral failure of *indifference* in a more palatable guise. It is a pretense to claim impartiality when the lack of engagement on a crucial issue is a lack of Christian love: What of the well-being of my neighbor? (Am I my brother's keeper?) Where truth and morally significant actions are at stake, we may not ignore the humanity of others without "crippling our own humanity." See Montague Brown, *The One Minute Philosopher* (Manchester, N.H.: Sophia Institute Press,

2001), 73. Bishop Fabian Bruskewitz instructed Catholics to be "careful that words like *caution* and *prudence* are not simply used as an excuse for inaction, inability, sloth, or cowardice, which prevents us from sharing a truth with others" (Presentation at Institute on Religious Life, April 10, 1999). Contemporary society has abolished sodomy laws that were based primarily on the religious consensus of the people (e.g., *Lawrence v. Texas*). It is pluralism that motivated an accommodation of a practice once punishable by law. Today no legal penalties apply to private homosexual acts that are consensual between persons of legal age. In that sense, the argument is that a "live and let live" approach has already been adopted by the culture. But a legal code that ignores the private behavior of adults is not warrant for transferring that same behavior to the status of a social model. For homosexual advocates to press for legal "marriage" to codify their liaison is hardly in the spirit of the "pluralism" they demand of others. To "live and let live" implies an effort on the part of the minority view to recognize an obligation toward the majority whose primary system of organization—families—is where they "live." Hence, "live and let live" stops where elevation of homosexual acts to the dignity of marriage is to devalue marriage for the majority of the pluralistic society. The tension in any multicultural society is to find a "livable" balance among diverse norms. For the majority, homosexual "marriage" is not a livable solution.

[27] James Q. Wilson, "Marriage Matters," *National Review*, October 9, 2000, 49–54.

[28] CCC 2357.

[29] William N. Eskridge, Jr. "The Emerging Menu of Quasi-Marriage Options" (http://writ.news.findlaw.com/commentary/20000707_eskridge.html).

[30] Maggie Gallagher, co-author of *The Case for Marriage* (New York: Doubleday, 2001) and editor of MarriageDebate.com, argues that "polygamy is not worse than gay marriage; it is better. At least polygamy, for all its ugly defects, is an attempt to secure stable mother-father families for children" ("The Stakes: Why We Need Marriage," www.nationalreview.com, July 14, 2003).

[31] Stanley Kurtz, "Beyond Gay Marriage" (www.weeklystandard.com/Content/Public/Articles/000/000/002/938xpsxy.asp).

[32] Ben Shapiro, "Gay Rights and the End of American Morality" (www.townhall.com/columnists/benshapiro/bs20030423.shtml).

[33] Kurtz, "Beyond Gay Marriage."

[34] Ibid.

[35] Roy Rivenburg, "Divided over Gay Marriage," *Los Angeles Times*, March 12, 2004, E1.

[36] Ibid.

[37] Ibid.

[38] Ibid.

[39] Ibid.

[40] Ibid.

[41] Naomi Shaefer, "His Better Halves: What's Wrong with Polygamy?" (www.opinionjournal.com/taste/?id=95001079).

[42] Rivenburg, "Divided over Gay Marriage."

[43] William J. Doherty et al., *Why Marriage Matters: Twenty-One Conclusions from the Social Scientists* (New York: Institute for American Values, 2002), 6.

[44] Maggie Gallagher and Linda Waite, *The Case for Marriage: Why Married People Are Happier and Better Off Financially* (New York: Doubleday, 2000); Glenn T. Stanton, *Why Marriage Matters: Reasons to Believe in Marriage in a Postmodern Society* (Colorado Springs: Pinon Press, 1997).

[45] Steven Stack and Ross Eshleman, "Marital Status and Happiness: A 17 Nation Study," *Journal of Marriage and the Family* 60 (May 1998): 527–38, quoted in Bridget E. Maher, *The Family Portrait*, (Washington: Family Research Council, 2002), 5.

[46] Pat Fagan et al., *The Positive Effects of Marriage: A Book of Charts* (www.heritage.org/Research/Features/Marriage/index.cfm). For more on the negative effects of divorce on children, see Judith S. Wallerstein, "The Long-Term Effects of Divorce on Children: A Review," *Journal of the American Academy of Child and Adolescent Psychiatry* 30, no. 3 (May 1991): 358–9.

[47] Rex Forehand et al., "Divorce/Divorce Potential and Interparental Conflict: The Relationship to Early Adolescent Social and Cognitive Functioning," *Journal of Adolescent Research* 1 (1986): 389–97; Carolyn Webster-Stratton, "The Relationship of Marital Support, Conflict and Divorce to Parent Perceptions, Behaviors and Childhood Conduct Problems," *Journal of Marriage and the Family* 51 (1989): 417–30; Ed Spruijt and Martijn de Goede, "Transition in Family Structure and Adolescent Well-being," *Adolescence* 32 (winter 1997): 897–911.

[48] Edward O. Laumann et al., *The Social Organization of Sexuality: Sexual Practices in the United States* (Chicago: University of Chicago Press, 1994), 364; Allan V. Horowitz et al., "Becoming Married and Mental Health: A Longitudinal Study of a Cohort of Young Adults," *Journal of Marriage and Family* 58 (November 1996): 895–907; Jennifer Marshall, "Marriage: What Social Science Says and Doesn't Say" (www.heritage.org/Research/Family/wm503.cfm).

[49] Waite and Gallagher, *The Case for Marriage*, 47–77.

[50] Karen S. Peterson, "Unhappily wed? Put off getting that divorce; study finds that waiting, working it out can pay off," *USA Today*, July 11, 2002.

[51] Linda Waite et al., *Does Divorce Make People Happy? Findings from a Study of Unhappy Marriages* (www.americanvalues.org/html/r-unhappy.html). Waite's team noted that divorce has uncontrolled consequences that include "the response of one's spouse to divorce; the reactions of children; potential disap-

pointments and aggravation in custody, child support, and visitation orders; new financial or health stresses for one or both parents; and new relationships or marriages," all of which mitigate against the happiness people anticipate will follow a divorce.

[52] Judith Wallerstein, Julia Lewis, and Sandra Blakeslee, *The Unexpected Legacy of Divorce* (New York: Hyperion, 2000), 295, 297.

[53] Norman Bales and Anne Bales, "Today's Blended Family Landscape," *All About Families*, April 26, 2000, 1-2; Lynn K. White and Alan Booth, "The Quality and Stability of Remarriages: The Role of Stepchildren," *American Sociological Review* 50, no. 5 (1985): 689-98; Frank F. Furstenberg, Jr., "Divorce and the American Family," *Annual Review of Sociology* 16 (1990): 379-403.

[54] Waite and Gallagher, *The Case for Marriage*, 148-9.

[55] Forehand et al., "Divorce/Divorce Potential and Interparental Conflict"; Webster-Stratton, "The Relationship of Marital Support, Conflict and Divorce to Parent Perceptions, Behaviors and Childhood Conduct Problems"; Spruijt and Goede, "Transition in Family Structure and Adolescent Well-being."

[56] Waite and Gallagher, *The Case for Marriage*, 129-40.

[57] Diana E. H. Russell, "The Prevalence and Seriousness of Incestuous Abuse: Stepfathers vs. Biological Fathers," *Child Abuse and Neglect* 8 (1984): 15-22; M. Wilson and M. Daly, "Risk of Maltreatment of Children Living with Stepparents," *Child Abuse and Neglect: Biosocial Dimensions*, ed. Gelles and Lancaster (New York: Aldine de Gruyer, 1987), 215-32; M. Konner, "Darwin's Truth, Jefferson's Vision: Sociobiology and the Politics of Human Nature," *The American Prospect* 45 (1999): 30-8.

[58] Wallerstein, "The Long-Term Effects of Divorce on Children," 358-9.

[59] Waite and Gallagher, *The Case for Marriage*, 148-9.

[60] John F. Harvey, O.S.F.S., *The Truth about Homosexuality* (San Francisco: Ignatius Press, 1996), 58.

[61] Susan Brinkman, "Gay Marriage: Who's Minding the Children?" *Catholic Standard and Times*, June 17, 2004. Part 5 of 6

[62] CCC 2357; Congregation for the Doctrine of the Faith, *Persona Humana* 8.

[63] P. Cameron and K. Cameron, "Homosexual Parents," *Adolescence* 31 (1996): 772.

[64] Timothy J. Daniel, "The Slippery Slope of Same-Sex Marriage" (www.frc.org/get.cfm?i=BC04C02).

[65] David P. McWhirter and Andrew M. Mattison, *The Male Couple: How Relationships Develop* (Englewood Cliffs: Prentice Hall, 1894), 252-3; M. Saghir and E. Robins, *Male and Female Homosexuality* (Baltimore: Williams and Wilkins, 1973), 225.

[66] A. P. Bell and M. S. Weinberg, *Homosexualities: A Study of Diversity Among*

Men and Women (New York: Simon and Schuster, 1978).

[67] Richard P. Fitzgibbons, "Origins and Healing of Homosexual Attractions and Behaviors" in Harvey, *The Truth about Homosexuality* (San Francisco: Ignatius Press, 1996), 317–8.

[68] Ibid.

[69] Ibid.

[70] Marvin Ellison, *Same-Sex Marriage? A Christian Ethical Analysis* (Cleveland, Ohio: Pilgrim Press, 2004), 116–7.

[71] Ibid., 127.

[72] Marshall Kirk and Hunter Madsen, *After the Ball* (New York: Plume, 1990), 367.

[73] Harvey, *The Truth about Homosexuality*, 234; Ellison, *Same Sex Marriage?*, 105.

[74] Ellison, *Same Sex Marriage?*, 108.

[75] Ibid., 104.

[76] David L. Tubbs and Robert P. George, "Redefining Marriage Away" (www.city-journal.org/html/14_3_redefining_marriage.html).

[77] The American Psychological Association adopted a resolution in favor of same-sex unions at its national convention in July 2004. The American Psychiatric Association endorsed same-sex partnerships in 2001. The latter first sought to normalize homosexuality in 1973 when it deleted homosexual practice as a disorder from its *Diagnostic and Statistical Manual of Mental Disorders*.

[78] H. Con. Res. 107, 106th Cong., 1st sess. (http://thomas.loc.gov/cgi-bin/bdquery/z?d106:HC00107:@@@D&summ2=m&).

[79] "The majority of the APA membership continued to view homosexuality as a pathology. A survey four years after the vote [1978] found that 69 percent of psychiatrists regarded homosexuality as a 'pathological adaptation.' A much more recent survey suggests that the majority of psychiatrists around the world continue to view same-sex behavior as signaling mental illness" (www.narth.com/docs/mentaldisorder.html).

[80] Charlotte J. Patterson, "Lesbian and Gay Parenting" (www.apa.org/pi/parent.html#I.%20SUMMARY%20OF%20RESEARCH%20FINDINGS).

[81] Ibid.

[82] Robert Lerner and Althea K. Nagai, *No Basis: What the Studies Don't Tell Us About Same Sex Parenting* (Washington: Ethics and Public Policy Center, 2001), 6.

[83] American College of Pediatricians, Mission Statement (www.acpeds.org). The statement reads in part, "We recognize the basic father-mother family unit, within the context of marriage, to be the optimal setting for childhood development."

[84] Ibid.

[85] American College of Pediatricians, "American College of Pediatricians Finds AAP's Sexual Orientation and Adolescents Report Troubling," press release, June 16, 2004.

[86] R. Green et al., "Lesbian Mothers and Their Children: A Comparison With Solo Parent Heterosexual Mothers and Their Children," *Archives of Sexual Behavior* 15 (1986): 167–83; P. A. Belcastro et al., "A Review of Data Based Studies Addressing the Effects of Homosexual Parenting on Children's Sexual and Social Functioning," *Journal of Divorce and Remarriage* 20 (1993): 105–22; B. Hoeffer, "Lesbian and Heterosexual Single Mothers: Influence of Their Child's Acquisition of Sex-Role Traits and Behavior," (dissertation, University of California), University of Michigan, Ann Arbor, 1979; D. L. Puryear, "Familial Experiences: A Comparison Between Children of Lesbian Mothers and the Children of Heterosexual Mothers," (Dissertation, University of California), University of Michigan, Ann Arbor, 1983; J. D. Kunin, "Predictors of Psychosocial and Behavioral Adjustment of Children: A Study Comparing Children Raised by Lesbian Parents to Children Raised by Heterosexual Parents," *Dissertation Abstracts International* 59 (1998): (6-B), 3094; G. A. Javaid, "The Children of Homosexual and Heterosexual Single Mothers," *Child Psychiatry and Human Development* 23 (1993): 235–48; K. Lewis, "The Children of Lesbians: Their Point of View," *Social Work* 23 (1980): 198–203.

[87] P. Cameron and K. Cameron, "Homosexual Parents," 757–66; P. Cameron and K. Cameron, "Homosexual Parents: A Comparative Forensic Study of Character and Harms to Children," *Psychological Reports* 82 (1998): 1155–91.

[88] Waite and Gallagher, *The Case for Marriage*, 129–40; Russell, "The Prevalence and Seriousness of Incestuous Abuse," in *Child Abuse and Neglect: Biosocial Dimensions*, ed. Gelles and Lancaster (New York: Aldine de Gruyer, 1987), 215–32.

[89] Jennifer Newton Reents, "Breastfeeding: for Dads?" *And Baby*, May-June 2003, 59–62.

[90] David Popenoe, *Life With Father: Compelling New Evidence That Fatherhood and Marriage Are Indispensable for the Good of Children and Society* (New York: Free Press, 1996), 139–63.

[91] Ibid.

[92] Ibid.

[93] David Blankenhorn, *Fatherless America: Confronting Our Most Urgent Social Problem* (New York: Basic Books, 1995).

[94] Maher, *The Family Portrait*, 85. "Instability of cohabiting relationships contributes to the more frequent depression among cohabitants. . . . Cohabitants who live with children or stepchildren are depressed more frequently

than married couples with children." Additionally, six- to twelve-year-olds in single parent families are more likely to lie, steal, destroy property, and choose troubled friends (118). For detailed analysis of multiple concerns in non-traditional families, see Susan L. Brown, "Child Well Being in Cohabiting Families," in Alan Booth and Ann C. Crouter, eds., *Just Living Together: Implications of Cohabitation on Children, Families, and Social Policy* (Mahwah, N.J.: Lawrence Erlbaum Associates, 2002), 173–87.

[95] Booth and Crouter, 89.

[96] Gallagher, "The Stakes"; see also "Statement of Five Dutch Social Science Professors on the Deterioration of Marriage in the Netherlands" (www.heritage.org/Research/Family/netherlandsstatement.cfm).

[97] Ibid.

[98] Ibid.

[99] The United Nations, after years of campaigning against the "population explosion," has now issued a warning to Europe about its crisis of depopulation. See also Pat Buchanan, *Death of the West* (New York: Thomas Dunne Books, 2001).

[100] Where immigration consists largely of persons from very different cultures or religious traditions, the host culture suffers civil tension as it tries to absorb the ways into the wider culture. The results often cause social discord.

[101] Gallagher, "The Stakes."

[102] The Holy See delegation at the United Nations consistently speaks against governmental programs designed to limit population via contraception and abortion. See Pope John Paul II, "Population Conference Draft Document Criticized" (www.ewtn.com/library/PAPALDOC/JP2POPUL.htm). The Pope said, "All propaganda and misinformation directed at persuading couples that they must limit their family to one or two children should be steadfastly avoided," and, citing *Centesimus Annus*, "It is necessary to go back to seeing the family as the sanctuary of life. The family is indeed sacred. . . . In the face of the so-called culture of death, the family is the heart of the culture of life." For its defense of families, the Holy See is regularly derided at U.N. international conferences. In 1999 at The Hague, a U.N. prepcom official remarked, "The Holy See continues to say that in matters of sexuality and reproduction, rights of the parents are supreme and the state should encourage this and not override it. We look forward to the day the Holy See comes into the twentieth century" (Mary Jo Anderson, "UN Frontline Report," *Voices* XIV, no. 1 [spring 1999]). Various U.N. conferences have promoted "sexual rights" that include all freedoms, including "orientation."

[103] CCC 2358.

[104] Cheryl Wetzstein, "Blacks angered by gays' metaphors" (www.washingtontimes.com/national/20040301-115928-8367r.htm).

Chapter 2: The Nature of Marriage

[1] Nicholas Berdyaev, *Freedom and the Spirit* (Freeport, N.Y.: Libraries Press, 1972).

[2] Richard M. Hogan and John M. LeVoir, *Covenant of Love: Pope John Paul II on Sexuality, Marriage and Family in the Modern World* (San Francisco: Ignatius Press, 1992), 47.

[3] Aristotle, *Ethics* VIII, xii. 7.

[4] CCC 2374

[5] Congregation for the Doctrine of the Faith, *Instruction on Respect for Human Life in Its Origin and on the Dignity of Procreation: Replies to Certain Questions of the Day (Donum Vitae)*, 2.

[6] Micheline M. Mathews-Roth, *Sexual Responsibility: A Doctor's Perspective* (Boston: Daughters of St. Paul, 1992), 17.

[7] Karol Wojtyla (John Paul II), *Love and Responsibility* (San Francisco: Ignatius Press, 1993). In particular, the chapter entitled "The Sexual Urge" communicates the joy of sex for the married couple. Here the Pope addresses with delicacy the need of the husband to be sensitive to the needs of the wife so that their intimate life is truly one of mutual pleasure.

[8] Hogan and LeVoir, *Covenant of Love*, 39, 44.

[9] Divorce rates in the U.S. in 1960 were 2.2 per 1,000 population and 5.3 per 1,000 by 1979. The rate declined to 4.0 per 1,000 by 2001 (divorcereform.org). It is important to note that statistics include the dissolution of second and third marriages.

[10] This philosophical divide from the traditional Judeo-Christian worldview was deftly outlined by Robert Reich, former secretary of labor in the Clinton administration: "The great conflict of the 21st century may be between the West and terrorism. But terrorism is a tactic, not a belief. The underlying battle will be between modern civilization and anti-modernist fanatics; between those who believe in the primacy of the individual and those who believe that human beings owe blind allegiance to a higher authority; between those who give priority to life in this world and those who believe that human life is no more than preparation for an existence beyond life; between those who believe that truth is revealed solely through Scripture and religious dogma, and those who rely primarily on science, reason, and logic." While Reich appears to be describing terrorism and radical Islamic beliefs, the context of these statements is "America as a Christian nation," where terrorism manifests as Christians who "promote the teaching of creationism in public schools, encourage school prayer, support anti-sodomy statutes, ban abortions, bar gay marriage, limit the use of stem cells, [and] reduce access to contraceptives" (Robert Reich, "Bush's

God" [www.prospect.org/web/page.ww?section=root&name=ViewPrint& articleId=7858]).

[11] B. F. Skinner, *Walden Two* (New York: Macmillan, 1976), 132–4. See discussion in Bryce J. Christiansen, *Utopia Against the Family* (San Francisco: Ignatius, 1990).

[12] Pope Paul VI, *Humanae Vitae* 17.

[13] Mercedes Arzu Wilson, "The Practice of Natural Family Planning Versus the Use of Artificial Birth Control: Family, Sexual and Moral Issues," *Catholic Social Science Review* 7 (2002): 1–30.

[14] Charlotte Hays, "Solving the Puzzle of Natural Family Planning," *Crisis*, December 2001, 15, 22. In addition to regulating births, natural planning methodologies are also used effectively by couples who want to conceive.

[15] HV 14.

[16] CCC 2368. The desire to space births may not be "motivated by selfishness" but may come after due consideration for a couple's particular circumstances.

[17] John Paul II, *Crossing the Threshold of Hope* (New York: Alfred A. Knopf, 1994), 207–8. The "culture of death" phrase has come to mean resorting to death to solve the problems of life: contraception, abortion, homosexuality, euthanasia, disease, poverty. It is fundamentally a worldview that sees life as the problem rather than the solution. "This culture is actively fostered by powerful cultural, economic, and political currents that encourage an idea of society excessively concerned with efficiency. Looking at the situation from this point of view, it is possible to speak in a certain sense of a war of the powerful against the weak: a life that would require greater acceptance, love, and care is considered useless or held to be an intolerable burden and is therefore rejected in one way or another. A person who, because of illness, handicap, or, more simply, just by existing, compromises the well-being or lifestyle of those who are more favored tends to be looked upon as an enemy to be resisted or eliminated. In this way a kind of 'conspiracy against life' is unleashed" (John Paul II, *Evangelium Vitae* 12).

[18] CCC 2366–71.

[19] Ibid., 2371.

[20] William B. Smith, "Morality and Sexuality: What the Church Teaches," in *Human Sexuality in Our Time*, ed. George A. Kelly (Boston: Daughters of St. Paul, 1979), 154.

[21] Mary Shivanandan, *Crossing the Threshold of Love: A New Vision of Marriage in the Light of John Paul II's Anthropology* (Washington: Catholic University of America Press, 1999), 118–20.

[22] Hays, "Solving the Puzzle of Natural Family Planning," 21.

[23] Ibid.

[24] CCC 2366–7.

[25] Bishop Paul S. Loverde (Arlington, Virginia), "Truths about Life, Love and Marriage" (www.catholicherald.com/loverde/2004homilies/homily0729.htm).

[26] In 1965, the Supreme Court case *Griswold v. Connecticut* invalidated a Connecticut anti-contraception law. *Griswold* overturned a Connecticut statute that read: "Any person who uses any drug, medicinal article, or instrument for the purpose of preventing conception shall be fined not less than fifty dollars or imprisoned not less than sixty days nor more than year or be both fined and imprisoned" (*General Statutes of Connecticut* [1958 rev.], 53-32 and 54-196).

[27] Ibid.

[28] Pope Pius XI, *Casti Connubii* 56.

[29] John A. Hardon, S.J., "Sex and Sanctity," in *Human Sexuality in Our Time*.

[30] Hays, "Solving the Puzzle of Natural Family Planning," 22.

[31] Researchers have linked abortion and breast cancer. The Association of American Physicians and Surgeons (AAPS) states: "The AAPS believes that patients have the right to give or withhold fully informed consent before undergoing medical treatment. This includes notification of potential adverse effects. While there is a difference of medical opinion concerning the abortion-breast cancer link, there is a considerable volume of evidence supporting this link, which is, moreover, highly plausible. We believe that a reasonable person would want to be informed of the existence of this evidence before making her decision" (www.abortionbreastcancer.com/press_releases/031103/). See also Patrick Carroll, "Trends and Risk Factors in English Breast Cancers," *British Journal of Cancer* 91, supplement 1 (July 2004): S24. Carroll reports that nulliparous abortions (abortions before a first full-term pregnancy) are "highly carcinogenic."

[32] Interestingly, most people still hope to get married "some day." "Over the past thirty years a consistent 96 percent of the American public has expressed a personal desire for marriage. Only 8 percent of American women consider remaining single ideal, a proportion that has not changed over the past twenty years. Almost three-quarters of adult Americans believe that 'marriage is a lifelong commitment that should not be ended except under extreme circumstances.' Even 81 percent of divorced and separated Americans still believe that marriage should be for life" (Maggie Gallagher, *The Abolition of Marriage: How We Destroy Lasting Love* [Washington: Regnery Publishing, 1996], 8). "By 1994, 40 percent of never-married women in their thirties had had an illegitimate child" (ibid., 5).

[33] "Many studies have found that those who live together before marriage have less-satisfying marriages and a considerably higher chance of eventually breaking up. One reason is that people who cohabit may be more skittish of

commitment and more likely to call it quits when problems arise. But in addition, the very act of living together may lead to attitudes that make happy marriages more difficult. . . . Cohabitants tend not to be as committed as married couples, and they are more oriented toward their own personal autonomy and less to the well-being of their partner" (David Popenoe, "The Top Ten Myths of Marriage" [http://health.discovery.com/centers/loverelationships/articles/marriage_myths.html]).

Also, studies consistently show that both married men and married women enjoy sex much more than single people do, particularly single women. See Edward O. Laumann et al., *The Social Organization of Sexuality*; Scott Stanley and Howard Markman, *Marriage in the 90s: A Nationwide Random Phone Survey* (Denver: PREP, Inc., 1997). Studies show that men find sex in a committed relationship far more satisfying than casual sex. Researchers have also observed that sexual infidelity hampers sexual satisfaction and general happiness in both sexes. See Robert G. Bringle and Bram P. Buunk, "Extradyadic Relationships and Sexual Jealousy," in *Sexuality in Close Relationships*, eds. K. McKinney and S. Sprecher (Hillsdale, N.J.: Lawrence Erlbaum Associates, 1991), 135–53.

[34] Yuanreng Hu and Noreen Goldman, "Mortality Differentials by Marital Status: An International Comparison," *Demography* 27, no. 2 (1990): 233–50.

[35] Elizabeth Schoenfeld, "Drumbeats for Divorce Reform" (www.policyreview.org/may96/homef.html).

[36] Gallagher, *Abolition of Marriage*, 11.

[37] CCC 2339.

[38] Ibid., 2359.

[39] "A spouse who occasions grave danger of soul or body to the other or to the children, or otherwise makes the common life unduly difficult, provides the other spouse with a reason to leave, either by a decree of the local ordinary or, if there is danger in delay, even on his or her own authority" (*Code of Canon Law* 1153 §1).

[40] "A marriage that is ratified and consummated cannot be dissolved by any human power or by any cause other than death" (ibid., 1141).

[41] "In all cases, when the reason for separation ceases, the common conjugal life is to be restored, unless otherwise provided by ecclesiastical authority" (ibid., 1153 §2). "The innocent spouse may laudably readmit the other spouse to the conjugal life, in which case he or she renounces the right to separation" (ibid., 1155).

Chapter 3: What Does the Church Teach?

[1] HV 12.

[2] Second Vatican Council, *Gaudium et Spes* 48.

[3] Congregation for the Doctrine of the Faith, *Considerations Regarding Proposals to Give Legal Recognition to Unions between Homosexual Persons* 2.

[4] Ibid., 3.

[5] Ibid.

[6] Ibid

[7] Ibid.

[8] Bishop Victor Galeone (St. Augustine, Florida), "Marriage: A communion of life and love," pastoral letter, November 8, 2003.

[9] CDF, *Considerations* 4.

[10] PH 8.

[11] "You shall not commit murder, you shall not commit adultery, you shall not commit pederasty, you shall not commit fornication, you shall not steal, you shall not practice magic, you shall not practice witchcraft, you shall not murder a child by abortion nor kill one that has been born" (*Didache* 2:2).

[12] Clement of Alexandria, *Exhortation to the Greeks* 2.

[13] Cyprian of Carthage, *Letters* 1:8.

[14] John Chrysostom, *Homilies on Titus* 5.

[15] CDF, *Considerations* II, 5.

[16] Ibid., 12.

[17] Ibid.

[18] Ibid., 5.

[19] Ibid.

[20] Ibid.

[21] Ibid.

[22] Ibid.

[23] Ibid., 10.

[24] Ibid.

[25] See EV 73 for situations in which a politician may be permitted to support proposals aimed at limiting the harm done by existing law that permits an objective moral evil.

[26] CCC 2358.

[27] Ibid., 2357.

[28] Ibid., 2358.

[29] Courage, an apostolate of the Roman Catholic Church, ministers to those with same-sex attractions and their loved ones. Endorsed by the Pontifical Council for the Family. See appendix II.

[30] Harvey, *The Truth about Homosexuality*, 172.

Chapter 4: What Does Medical Science Say?

[1] Dale O'Leary, *The Gender Agenda*, (Lafayette, La.: Vital Issues Press, 1997), 161.

[2] *Oxford Dictionary*, new edition (New York: Oxford University Press, 1992).

[3] Congregation for the Doctrine of the Faith, *Letter to the Bishops of the Catholic Church on the Collaboration of Men and Women in the Church and in the World* 3.

[4] Joyce A. Little, *The Church and the Culture War* (San Francisco: Ignatius Press, 1995), 102-3.

[5] Richard P. Fitzgibbons, "Gender Identity Disorder in Children" (www.narth.com/docs/fitz.html).

[6] Kenneth Zucker and Susan Bradley, *Gender Identity Disorder and Psychosexual Problems in Children and Adolescents* (New York: Guilford Press, 1995).

[7] Jeffrey Satinover, "How Might Homosexuality Develop? Putting the Pieces Together" (www.narth.com/docs/pieces.html).

[8] Richard Friedman, *Male Homosexuality: A Contemporary Psychoanalytic Perspective*, quoted in Dale O'Leary, "Childhood Experiences of Homosexual Men" (www.fathersforlife.org/dale/child1.html).

[9] Moberly, "Homosexuality and the Truth," 30-3.

[10] "The American Psychological Association and the American Psychiatric Association have officially protested what they view as a misrepresentation of their position on pedophilia. Their protesting statements affirm laws against sexual relationships between adults and children. Fair enough, but that is somewhat beside the point.

"While avoiding obvious legal landmines, the associations have been moving since the 1970s toward legitimating homosexuality, along with pedophilia and other 'paraphiliac' behavior (e.g., sadomasochism), in that they are no longer listed as mental disorders unless they cause distress or impair the social functioning of those who indulge in such behavior. The question is not whether the associations favor decriminalizing pedophilia. They do not. But their area of presumed competence is mental disorders, not changing the law. A change has been made in the definition of mental disorders, and their protest would be made credible only by rescinding the change. One might surmise that practitioners of 'man-boy love' do not feel distress about what they do, nor, within that subculture, is their social functioning impaired. It is accurate to say that the associations appear to be on a course toward 'normalizing' behavior that previously was judged to be perverse and disordered and is still illegal. Whatever their intentions, it is foreseeable that such a course might at some point have a bearing on changes in the law. Although the associations deplore it, the reality is that mental disorder bears a social stigma. Officially removing that stigma is a step toward normalizing certain actions, or at least delegitimating objections to them, which is much the same thing" (Richard John Neuhaus, "The Public Square," *First Things*, February 2000, 90.)

[11] Moberly, "Homosexuality and the Truth," 30.

[12] Charles Socarides, "Sexual Politics and Scientific Logic: The Issue of Homosexuality" (www.geocities.com/kidhistory/homopolo.htm).

[13] William J. Bennett, "Gay Marriage: Not a Very Good Idea," (www.catholiceducation.org/articles/homosexuality/ho0013.html).

[14] C. Bagley and P. Tremblay, "Suicidal Behaviors in Homosexual and Bisexual Males," *Crisis* 18 (1997): 24–34.

[15] R. A. Garofalo et al., "The Associations between Health Risk Behaviors and Sexual Orientation Among a School-Based Sample of Adolescents," *Pediatrics* 101 (1998): 895–902.

[16] Lesbians are five times more likely to be classified as heavy drinkers than heterosexual women. See Alison L. Diamant et al., "Health Behaviors, Health Status, and Access to and Use of Health Care," *Archives of Family Medicine* 9 (November-December 2000): 1048, quoted in Dailey and Sprigg, *Getting It Straight*, 86.

[17] Joanne Hall, "Lesbians Recovering from Alcoholic Problems," *Nursing Research* 43 (1994): 238–44, quoted in Dailey and Sprigg, *Getting It Straight*, 107.

[18] R. Herrell et al., "A Co-Twin Study in Adult Men," *Archives of General Psychiatry* 56 (1999): 867–74; D. M. Fergusson, J. Horwood, and A. L. Beautrais, "Is Sexual Orientation Related to Mental Health Problems and Suicidality in Young People?" *Archives of General Psychiatry* 56 (1999): 876–80; M. J. Bailey, "Homosexuality and Mental Illness," *Archives of General Psychiatry* 56 (1999): 883–4.

[19] P. Cameron and K. Cameron, "Homosexual Parents," *Adolescence* 31 (1996): 757–76.

[20] Ibid.

[21] Laura Dean et al., "Lesbian, Gay, Bisexual and Transgender Health: Findings and Concerns," *Journal of the Gay and Lesbian Medical Association* 4, no. 3 (2000): 101–51; Centers for Disease Control, *Weekly Report* 53 (42): 985–8 (www.cdc.gov/mmwr/preview/mmwrhtml/mm5342a2.htm).

[22] P. E. Newman, "Sporadic Transmission of Hepatitis C" (http://hepatitis-c.de/transmit.htm); Sammy Saab and Paul Martin, "Tests for Acute and Chronic Viral Hepatitis" (www.postgradmed.com/issues/2000/02_00/saab.htm); see also www.natap.org/2004/HCV/090704_01.htm.

[23] Bell and Weinberg, *Homosexualities*, 308–9.

[24] Medical Institute for Sexual Health, *Health Implications Associated with Homosexuality* (Austin, Tex.: Medical Institute for Sexual Health, 1999), 55, quoted in Dailey and Sprigg, *Getting It Straight*, 80–1. See also Jack Morin, *Anal Pleasure and Health: A Guide for Men and Women* (San Francisco: Down There Press, 1998), 220.

[25] R. J. Ablin and R. Stein-Werblowsky, "Sexual Behavior and Increased Anal Cancer," *Immunology and Cell Biology* 75, no. 2 (1997): 181–3.

[26] Katherine Fethers et al., "Sexually Transmitted Infections and Risk Behaviors in Women Who Have Sex with Women," *Sexually Transmitted Infections* 76 (2000): 348, quoted in Dailey and Sprigg, *Getting It Straight*, 84–5.

[27] Bell and Weinberg, *Homosexualities*, 308–9.

[28] A *Nursing Research* article reports that "like most problem drinkers, 91 percent of participants [in the study] had abused other drugs as well as alcohol, and many reported compulsive difficulties with food" (Hall, "Lesbians Recovering from Alcoholic Problems," quoted in Dailey and Sprigg, *Getting It Straight*, 107). "Along with being less likely to have been pregnant, other studies have shown that lesbians in general may be slightly heavier than heterosexual women. Heavier women have a higher risk of developing breast cancer after menopause. Lesbians are also more likely to have smoked cigarettes than heterosexual women—another risk factor for breast cancer. . . . Lesbians are at higher risk of breast, cervical, and ovarian cancers because they are less likely to have children by age thirty, if at all" (Richard A. Zmuda, "Lesbians and Cancer Risk" [www.cancerpage.com/news/article.asp?id=1547]).

[29] J. Bradford et al., "National Lesbian Health Care Survey: Implications for Mental Health Care," *Journal of Consulting and Clinical Psychology* 62 (1994): 239, quoted in Dailey and Sprigg, *Getting It Straight*, 87. See also "Ten Things Gay Men Should Discuss with Their Health Care Providers" (www.glma.org/news/releases/n02071710gaythings.html).

[30] J. B. Lehmann, C. U. Lehmann, and P. J. Kelly, "Development and Health Care Needs of Lesbians," *Journal of Women's Health* 7 (1998): 379–88.

[31] J. Bradford et al., "National Lesbian Health Care Survey."

[32] A. Dean Byrd, "In Their Own Words: Gay Activists Speak About Science, Morality, Philosophy" (www.narth.com/docs/innate.html).

[33] Ibid.

[34] Catholic Medical Association, "Homosexuality and Hope" (www.cathmed.org/publications/homosexuality.html).

[35] Simon LeVay, "A Difference in Hypothalamic Structure between Heterosexual and Homosexual Men," *Science* 253 (August 1991): 1036.

[36] William Masters, Virginia E. Johnson, and Robert C. Kolodny, *Human Sexuality* (Boston: Little Brown and Co., 1985), 411–2.

[37] Dailey and Sprigg, *Getting It Straight*, 2–3.

[38] William Byne and Bruce Parsons, "Human Sexual Orientation: The Biologic Theories Reappraised," *Archives of General Psychiatry* 50 (1993): 228–39.

[39] "In fact Bruce Voeller (1990) claims to have originated the 10 percent estimate as part of the modern-day gay-rights movement's campaign in the late 1970s to convince politicians that 'We [gays and lesbians] Are Everywhere.' At the same time, Voeller was chair of the National Gay Task Force" (Edward O. Laumann et al., 289, n. 7, citing Bruce Voeller, "Some Uses and Abuses of the Kinsey Scale," in *Homosexuality–Heterosexuality: Concepts of Sexual Orientation*, ed. David P. McWhirter, Stephanie A. Saunders, and June Machover Reinisch [New York: Oxford University Press, 1990]).

[40] Robert T. Michael et al., *Sex in America: A Definitive Survey* (Boston: Little Brown and Co., 1994), 176–7, quoted in Dailey and Sprigg, *Getting It Straight*, 42.

[41] Matthew V. Pruitt, "Size Matters: A Comparison of Anti- and Pro-Gay Organizations' Estimates of the Size of the Gay Population," *Journal of Homosexuality* 42 (2002): 26–7.

[42] Judith Reisman, *Kinsey: Crimes and Consequences*, 2nd ed. (Crestwood, Ky.: Institute for Media Education, 2000); see also Judith Reisman et al., *Kinsey, Sex, and Fraud* (Lafayette, La.: Lochinvar and Huntington House, 1990).

[43] Patrick Rogers, "How Many Gays Are There?" *Newsweek*, February 15, 1993, 46.

[44] Reisman, *Kinsey: Crimes and Consequences*, 205.

[45] "2,400 lawmakers warn of Kinsey Influence" (www.worldnetdaily.com/news/article.asp?ARTICLE_ID=39290).

[46] Richard Fitzgibbons and Joseph Nicolosi, "Gender Identity Disorder" (www.christianity.com/partner/Article_Display_Page/0,,PTID4211%7CCHID102755%7CCIID479588,00.html).

[47] Satinover, "How Might Homosexuality Develop?"

Chapter 5: What Does the Bible Say?

[1] Second Vatican Council, *Dignitatis Humanae*.

[2] Second Vatican Council, *Lumen Gentium* 17.

[3] CCC 2032

[4] Ibid., 2447

[5] This is a view held by John Boswell, who theorized that it was the rape of the two angels that angered God. But Boswell's theory is quickly undone by Genesis 18:20, where God had already planned to destroy the cities—their sin was legendary *before* the angelic visitors were sent to Sodom to investigate

(John Boswell, *Christianity, Social Tolerance, and Homosexuality* [Chicago: University of Chicago Press, 1980], 93).

[6] Rabbinic literature lists "same-sex intercourse among the sins of the generation of the Flood" (Robert A. J. Gagnon, *The Bible and Homosexual Practice* [Nashville: Abingdon Press, 2001], 75, note 95).

[7] William Whiston, trans., *The New Complete Works of Josephus*, Jewish Antiquities, book I, ch. 11, 1–3.

[8] Ibid., 57–8.

[9] Ibid., 146–54.

Chapter 6: Political Considerations

[1] The National Association for Research and Therapy of Homosexuality offers "effective psychological therapy available to all homosexual men and women who seek change." See appendix II for contact information.

[2] Joseph Nicolosi, *Reparative Therapy of Male Homosexuality: A New Clinical Approach* (Northvale, N.J.: Jason Aronson, Inc., 1991).

[3] Robert L. Spitzer, "Can Some Gay Men and Lesbians Change Their Sexual Orientation? 200 Participants Reporting a Change from Homosexual to Heterosexual Orientation," *Archives of Sexual Behavior* 32, no. 5 (October 2003): 403–17.

[4] Nicolosi, *Reparative Therapy of Male Homosexuality*, xv.

[5] Marshall Kirk and Hunter Madsen, *After the Ball* (New York: Plume [Penguin Group], 1990), 183.

[6] Ibid., 189.

[7] *Lawrence v. Texas*, 000 U.S. 02-102 (2003).

[8] Ibid.

[9] "U.N. Resolution to globalize 'gay' rights" (www.wnd.com/news/article.asp?ARTICLE_ID=36916).

Index